OBOE TECHNIQUE

By the same author

A BOOK OF SCALES FOR THE OBOE

Uniform with this volume

FLUTE TECHNIQUE
by F. B. Chapman
Third Edition

CLARINET TECHNIQUE
by Frederick Thurston

BASSOON TECHNIQUE
by Archie Camden

HORN TECHNIQUE
by Gunther Schuller

RECORDER TECHNIQUE
by A. Rowland-Jones

ORCHESTRAL PERCUSSION
TECHNIQUE
by James Blades

Oboe Technique

BY EVELYN ROTHWELL

1368

Second Edition

LONDON
OXFORD UNIVERSITY PRESS
NEW YORK   TORONTO
1962

Oxford University Press, Amen House, London, E.C.4

GLASGOW NEW YORK TORONTO MELBOURNE WELLINGTON
BOMBAY CALCUTTA MADRAS KARACHI LAHORE DACCA
CAPE TOWN SALISBURY NAIROBI IBADAN ACCRA
KUALA LUMPUR HONG KONG

First published 1953

Second edition 1962

Printed in Great Britain by
The Camelot Press Ltd., London and Southampton

To my Friend and Colleague in the U.S.A.
WHITNEY TUSTIN

PREFACE

In any art, the achievement of a fine technique should never be considered an end in itself. It is, however, an essential means to an end, for it is obvious that no artist can fully express himself without having technical mastery over his means of expression. Technique means *control* over all the muscles concerned. Many woodwind players talk of it only in relation to the tongue and the fingers, but since real command of the breath and embouchure is certainly as important as lingual and digital dexterity, I have tried to explain how to achieve fine control over the muscles needed for every aspect of oboe technique.

Since an unsatisfactory oboe or a faulty reed can so vitally affect a player's performance, I have included chapters on the care of the instrument and on reeds.

At the end of the book is an Appendix on playing the cor anglais, and another giving a list of solos and chamber music for the oboe and cor anglais.

My grateful thanks are due to my husband and to the friends who have so kindly read and commented upon the manuscript and proofs of this little book, particularly to Janet Craxton, Geraldine Hedges, Dr. Reginald Hilton and Whitney Tustin, whose constructive criticisms have been of the greatest value to me.

E. R.

Autumn, 1952

PREFACE TO THE SECOND EDITION

In this edition I have made several additions and alterations to the text to amplify and clarify certain points. Appendix III (a list of music for the oboe, oboe d'amore, and cor anglais) has been brought up to date and greatly enlarged.

E. R.

Spring, 1962

CONTENTS

IV. FINGER CONTROL

V. THE INSTRUMENT AND ITS CARE

VI. REEDS AND THEIR CARE

VII. PRACTICE

HOW TO PRODUCE A SOUND FROM THE OBOE

Though this book is intended primarily for amateurs and students who are actually learning the oboe, it is possible that a few of those who read it may not yet have begun to play. It is for them that this Introduction has been written; the chapters which follow will be of far more interest to those who have at least tried to produce a few notes from the oboe.

1. *Assembling the instrument*

The oboe consists of four parts:

(*a*) The reed (which is, in effect, the mouthpiece) consisting of two blades of scraped cane bound on to a staple—tube—of metal and cork.

(*b*) The top joint.

(*c*) The bottom joint.

(*d*) The bell.

First fit the top and bottom joints together, using a gentle screwing action, making sure that the central holes and plates are in a straight line, and that any keywork connections at the sides are properly aligned. Then put the bell on to the bottom joint—again ensuring that the metal connection is correctly placed. Finally insert the reed into the oboe, the staple pushed right home into the socket in the top joint, with the flat blades of the reed parallel to the finger holes.

2. *Making a sound with the reed only*

Before trying to make a sound on the oboe, moisten the reed, and try to produce a squeak from it in the following way.

Relax your mouth, allowing your lips and your teeth to be slightly apart. Now pull your lower jaw and chin down and back a little, and roll both your lips over your teeth. Take in a deep breath and hold it: put the reed in the middle of your mouth between your lips so that about a third to a half of the cane is covered by them, holding it firmly so that no air escapes from around it. The muscles round your mouth should contract slightly to help the lips achieve this control, and you may find it helpful to think of your mouth in a position a little like this ‿, rather than ⁀. Now say 'Ter', with your tongue against the tip of the reed instead of against the roof of your mouth as when speaking, which will start the reed vibrating freely: simultaneously exhale your breath slowly, and you should produce a squeaking sound.

3. *Playing a note*

The beginner on the oboe always has difficulty in covering the rings and holes with the fingers so that no leakage of air occurs. I suggest, therefore, that the first note you try to play should be a B natural in the middle octave, since only one finger is needed—plus the left thumb on the thumb-plate system.[1] When you can squeak the reed quite easily, put it into the instrument and go through the procedure described above, fingering as follows. Put your right thumb under the thumb-rest on the back of the bottom joint to support the oboe, allowing the first three fingers of the right hand to hover over the three rings and/or key-plates down the bottom joint, and the fourth finger over the three keys on the lower right-hand side of this joint.

Place your left thumb on the thumb-plate, the lower of the two keys at the back of the top joint (or if you use the Conservatoire system,[1] just below the one key there which is the first octave key).[2] Put the first finger of the left hand on the key-plate which is level with the thumb, the second and third fingers over the next two rings or key-plates down the top joint, and the fourth finger over the keys on the left-hand side of the oboe.

With your fingers placed thus, the thumb and first finger of the left hand held firm and the rest ready for action, you should sound the middle B natural. Then you can add the second finger of the left hand on the next large ring or plate, which will give you A, and so going down in the scale of D major. You will find that this way of beginning to play is

[1] Systems of fingering are discussed in Chapter V.
[2] On some oboes there are two keys—the first and the extra third octave keys.

easier than trying to start from the bottom, as the lower notes involve using more fingers, and are harder to produce.

Some of you who have read this Introduction may be hoping to teach yourself the oboe. Even if your intention is only to become an amateur player of the most limited capacity, let me advise you to take *at least* a few reliable lessons to put you on the right track, and an occasional one thereafter to keep you on it. You will thus get so much more pleasure from playing, and more value from the rest of this book.

BREATH CONTROL

Breathing is a natural process essential to life, and in our normal existence the breathing muscles inflate and deflate the lungs regularly and continuously without any conscious thought or effort on our part. In playing a wind instrument this regular periodical breathing must give way to the demands of the instrument and the musical phrases; consequently the frequency and extent of the inhalations and exhalations must be governed by the player. At first this control may be difficult to achieve, but when the breathing muscles are properly developed and trained their controlling actions should be as easy and as un-selfconscious as normal breathing.

The general principle of making any wind instrument sound is the same for all of them. The air stream breathed into the instrument must be made to vibrate and to vary in pressure by going through a mouthpiece controlled by the player's lips. The air stream needed varies in volume and pressure according to the instrument; of them all, the oboe uses the *smallest* amount of air at the *highest* pressure. Its double-reed mouthpiece has only a tiny opening and will therefore admit only a very small air stream, but in order to make the reed mouthpiece vibrate, this air stream must go through it very quickly, i.e. at a high pressure.

Variations in dynamics and in pitch on the oboe, as on all wind instruments, are made by altering the volume and the pressure of the air stream. These alterations are controlled by the *closely co-ordinated* actions of the breathing muscles and the embouchure[1] muscles. The breathing muscles govern the volume of the air stream, and the embouchure muscles control its pressure by adjusting the opening of the reed. (This chapter is concerned only with the actions of the breathing muscles; the functions of the embouchure muscles will be fully discussed in Chapter II.)

Since, as I have just explained, the oboe player uses a small amount of air at a high pressure (as compared with

[1] The word 'embouchure' is fully defined at the beginning of Chapter II.

the speaker or singer who uses a larger amount of air at a relatively low pressure), controlling the breath while playing the oboe is more exacting than breathing in normal life. If you take in a deep breath and breathe out slowly and then quickly or vice versa, you will be altering the volume of the air stream, and you will naturally find this quite easy. Altering the volume of the air stream while playing the oboe is not quite such a simple matter, although the process is the same. The reason is that the air stream used is *always* very small, even at its largest, and so the alterations to it must be *very* slight and sensitive: therefore the muscles controlling the breath must be particularly finely developed and trained. While some students, particularly young ones, acquire adequate breath control naturally as they master the oboe, many others retard the progress of their playing because they do not develop their breathing muscles sufficiently for the demands of the instrument.

It is vital to realize that IN ORDER TO PRODUCE A FINE TONE ON THE OBOE, YOU MUST HAVE A HIGH PRESSURE OF AIR AVAILABLE: THIS MEANS THAT YOU MUST LEARN TO INHALE IN THE RIGHT WAY.

1. *Inhaling a complete breath*

In normal life comparatively few people breathe *completely*. When you begin playing the oboe it is vitally important to learn this. A complete breath is one in which the air taken in is distributed to *all* parts of the lungs by *all* the muscles used to expand the chest. You can breathe in this way for inhaling a large or a small amount of air. First practise the complete FULL breath to develop your muscles. Stand erect, breathe in steadily through your nose and, just for the moment, learn how to inhale in three stages. (1) Fill the lower part of your lungs—the most important part, which holds the most air—by using your diaphragm. A well-known wind player helps his pupils by telling them to feel as if they were breathing with their stomach. Put your hand in front just above your navel: as you breathe in slowly and deeply you should feel the muscles pushing your hand out. (2) Fill the middle part of your lungs by expanding your lower ribs and breastbone. Put your hands on your ribs either side, and then on the front and back, to feel your chest expanding. (3) Fill the upper part of your lungs—NOT by raising your shoulders but by protruding the higher part of your chest. In this final stage of the complete breath, the lower part of the abdomen will draw in slightly to support the lungs.[1]

I have described the complete breath in three stages to try to explain how you use *all* your breathing muscles, but now you must learn to inhale completely in one steady continuous movement. Having taken in your breath, hold it for a few seconds (only as long as is comfortable without straining); then let it out slowly and steadily—drawing in the abdomen a little and lifting it upwards slowly as the air leaves the lungs. Then relax. Don't overdo your breathing practise. Just try to take in and let out one or two full complete breaths occasionally during the day. It will soon become easy and natural to breathe in this way and once you have learnt to do so, remember that a complete breath is one which distributes a large or a small amount of air to all parts of your lungs—a complete breath need not *necessarily* be a full breath.

The other vital point to realize is that *you must learn to exhale the breath quickly as well as to inhale it deeply*, and the following section should make it clear to you how vital it is to learn to breathe out stale air before breathing in fresh.

2. *'Taking a breath'*

While the muscles used for controlling breathing are the same for the speaker or singer as for the oboe player, the term 'taking a breath' means something rather different. As I have already said, to produce a good sound on the oboe with the maximum of control but with the minimum of effort, you must have a high pressure of air available. You must take in—*and hold while playing*—a good full lungful of air; in other words, the chest must be well expanded. But since the opening of the reed is so small that it can let through only a tiny amount of air at a time, the oboe player who becomes in common parlance 'out of breath', actually has his lungs almost *full*, but of stale, nearly deoxygenated air, from which the working

[1] Students past the very beginning stages may feel that it would be helpful to know a little more about the actions of their breathing muscles. They can read the brief explanation given in Appendix I.

muscles have used the oxygen. The player's urgent need then is to expel this, before literally 'taking a breath' in. The action of breathing for the oboe player is in fact a double one— letting out the old air and taking in the new. Since so little air is used, the exhalation from the lungs while playing must be very slow and must be finely controlled by the muscles of the diaphragm and the abdominal wall. These muscles should feel taut to the touch as you play. To get rid of the stale air in your lungs with the maximum speed and efficiency, the abdominal muscles must *push* out the air. Use them for this purpose just as you do when you cough or sneeze: you can feel their actions by putting your hand on your abdomen while you cough.

When you have finished this chapter you should realize how important it is always to 'take a breath' properly, push- ing out the stale air as thoroughly as possible before breathing in the new. It is vital to use every opportunity to get rid of the accumulation of carbon dioxide in your lungs, to renew the supply of oxygen in the body, and to relieve the pressure on the muscles while playing. On that account it is wise to 'take a breath' whenever the opportunity arises, whether it happens to be urgently needed at that moment or not. There are occasions when there is not time for the complete double action, and it is then often advisable to expel a little air and to continue playing with the chest less fully expanded for a very short while, before taking in more air at the next brief oppor- tunity. For this limited time the abdominal muscles should be able to maintain the air pressure necessary to prevent the tone deteriorating, even with the smaller amount of air available.[1] This naturally requires fine control, and the follow- ing exercise may be usefully practised in all keys, and also over

[1] There is a school of thought which advocates *always* inhaling very little air before playing, so that there is less to *ex*hale when the need arises. This may be an advantage, but in my opinion it is far outweighed by the dis- advantages of this method. Since the chest is only slightly expanded, there is a reduced pressure of air available. The abdominal muscles, helped by the throat muscles, must try to compensate for this by *forcing* the air up, rather than letting it flow slowly but freely from the chest to the reed, as in the correct way of playing. The reduced pressure so obtained affects the tone, which lacks resonance and quality, and the limited breathing makes playing tiring and unhealthy because too little oxygen is taken into the system to compensate for the muscular effort required to produce and control the sound. I consider it a method of playing to be avoided.

two octaves. (The intake of breath is marked V and the expelling of it O.)

A good example of the practical application of this method of breathing occurs at figure 3 in the first movement of the Strauss Oboe Concerto.[1]

3. *Developing the breathing muscles*

Since well-developed breathing muscles are so necessary a part of the oboe player's technical equipment, beginners would be wise to encourage their development by these simple exercises. (*a*) Inhale a complete full breath as described on page 5: hold it a few seconds. (Practice will make it progressively easier to hold the breath for increasing lengths of time, but never strain to hold it longer than is quite comfortable.) Now close up your lips as if for a whistle (or, if you like, for an oboe embouchure): don't puff out your cheeks. Push out a little air with vigour, rather as if you were playing a sforzando on the oboe. Stop for a moment, holding the breath; then exhale a little more air vigorously through your pursed lips. Repeat until the air is exhaled as completely as possible. Relax.

(*b*) Taking your own pulse beat as your 'Tempo', breathe in steadily for 4 beats, hold your breath for 2 beats, exhale it in 4 beats, wait for 2 beats and repeat twice. Gradually you will be able to increase the number of beats, but never tire

[1] Published by Boosey and Hawkes.

yourself and always keep the rhythm. Increase to 6 beats in, 3 held, 6 out, 3 wait: then 8, 4, 8, 4, and so on.

Repeat exercise (*a*).

Do these exercises when you can, especially before and after practising, preferably before an open window or in the fresh air.

4. *The effect of oboe playing on the health*

Provided that your heart and lungs are sound (it is a wise precaution to get a doctor to check them) and that you breathe properly, oboe playing should not be in the least injurious to your health. On the contrary, breathing deeply and developing your breathing muscles so fully should improve your general physical condition.[1]

Before beginners have learnt to control the breath, they may tend to push too much air through the tiny opening of the reed, thus producing a coarse and uncontrolled sound and using a great deal of air, but as the muscles develop and learn to 'hold the breath back', it should become quite easy to play a long phrase without 'taking a breath'. But because of the physical strain involved in controlling the small air stream, continuous playing is tiring and hard to control. Beginners sometimes experience a slight feeling of giddiness, and occasionally headache, after playing the oboe for a little while. There may be two causes for these troubles. (*a*) Not taking a sufficiently deep breath before playing, or trying to play too long without properly 'taking a breath'. The working muscles are using up the oxygen in the body, and if only a small amount of air has been inhaled the oxygen in it will soon be exhausted, and the player will begin to suffer from the lack of it. The same thing will happen if you try to make the air last too long, or if you fail to push out the stale air before taking in the fresh. (*b*) Using a reed with too strong a resistance to the pressure of the air stream, i.e. a reed which does not vibrate easily. A strong reed will require a high

[1] There is a charmingly apposite quotation from *The Castel of Helthe*, written by Thomas Elyot in 1533. He recommends the playing of shawms (the forerunners of the oboe, and primitive versions of it) as a healthful exercise, because 'they requyre moche wynde, and are thus beneficial to the entrayles which lye underneathe the mydreffe'. Substitute 'much control of wind' for 'moche wynde', and his advice still holds good today!

pressure to make it sound. Too high a pressure within the lungs will tend to slow down the circulation of blood through the smallest vessels. There will therefore be a deficiency in the blood flow to and from the heart. Provided that the heart and lungs are sound, these minor physical distresses should soon disappear as the muscular control develops. Until then, always take in a really deep breath before playing, never try to play too long without 'taking a breath' properly, use a reed which will vibrate easily (chosen by your teacher) and do breathing exercises regularly.

5. *The importance of posture*

In order that you may breathe naturally and easily, you must stand or sit in an upright—though never stiff—position. Your chest should be raised, shoulders naturally straight (*not* lifted), and your head up—chin well in and neck straight. Your elbows should be held away from your body, the wrists fairly flat, so that your arms cannot cramp your chest expansion and in order that your fingers may lie in a good position on the oboe. The angle at which the instrument is held away from the body must vary according to the individual and the method of playing used, but the average is at an angle of approximately 45 degrees. (The importance of the position of the oboe in regard to the embouchure will be discussed later.) Keep both your feet firmly on the ground, not too far apart, so that you are steady and well-balanced. Divide your practice time between playing standing up and sitting down, so that you are equally at home either way. If you are sitting sit well into your chair (it is usually more comfortable to use a straight-backed hard-seated one, not too low and without arms), supporting the small of your back against the back of the chair and keeping both feet flat on the floor. Do not get into the habit of playing sitting with your legs crossed. This may encourage you to slump and constrict your breathing muscles, and also to rest the oboe on your knee instead of balancing it properly on your right thumb, so that in time you will find it almost impossible to play while standing. Whether sitting or standing, never lean forward or slouch back. Try not to move too much when you are playing. For instance, exaggerated shakings of the head, or pumping up and down with the arms, can become disturbing and annoying to those watching you play.

6. *Dynamics*

To increase the volume of sound, you must increase the volume of the air stream. (Breathe out more quickly.)

To decrease the volume of sound, the opposite applies: decrease the volume of the air stream. (Breathe out more slowly.)

As I said at the beginning of this chapter, dynamics (also intonation) are controlled by the *co-ordinated* actions of the breathing and embouchure muscles. This subject will therefore be discussed more fully in Chapter II, after the functions of the embouchure have been explained.

7. *Bad habits*

(*a*) *Wrong control of the air stream.* Of all bad habits, perhaps the hardest to cure is that of trying to control the volume of the air stream with the throat muscles, instead of with the breathing muscles. Do not let the breath out too quickly, and then hold back part of this air stream from the reed by contracting the throat muscles. Always use the abdominal muscles to control the exhalation, so that you never breathe out a larger air stream than is needed. NEVER use the throat muscles as a dam to hold back forcefully an overlarge and ill-controlled air stream, nor to *push* the air through the reed. This incorrect method of graduating the volume of the air stream will produce an uneven and uncontrolled tone. Also, this way of playing frequently encourages the use of a hectically fast vibrato (mentioned in the next section).

(*b*) '*Bulging.*' Beware always of the very common bad habit of making a 'bulge', i.e. a little <>, on each note, or over every few notes. It is a monotonous, niggling form of expression, which is unmusical, and maddening to the listener. Unfortunately, it seems fatally easy for oboe players to acquire this bad habit, and you must listen to yourself most carefully and critically to avoid doing so. Think always of the curve and climax of the phrase you are playing and let the sound flow through and over it.

(*c*) *Snorting and grunting while playing.* These unattractive sounds are made when the player tries to get rid of stale air through the nose—usually without taking the reed from the mouth, and often while actually playing.[1] Though advanced players find it helpful on occasions to use the nose for breathing, many beginners do this because they are afraid of disturbing their embouchure, and thus they form a bad habit which is often very hard to cure. Try to make a fresh embouchure when you take a fresh breath, and use the *mouth* for breathing in and out. Incidentally this will improve your embouchure control, because the muscles will be more sensitive and flexible after their momentary relaxation, and you will find that forming your embouchure will soon become so natural and automatic that your fear of disturbing it will vanish. If you are taking a breath hurriedly you need not take the reed right out of your mouth; just let it rest on your relaxed lower lip.

(*d*) *Breaking off the end of a phrase abruptly to take a breath.* Never do this; always round off, or fade out, the end of the phrase with a tiny diminuendo. Even if you *have* to cut the last note of a phrase a fraction short in order to give yourself time to breathe, it will be so much less disturbing to the musical line, and to the listener, not to cut that note off sharply. Always let the tone fade away by stopping the breath, as you do naturally when talking. Hold the abdominal muscles steady until the sound has ceased, and then relax. Unless an exaggeratedly short note is required (see Chapter III, section 2), never stop a note by closing the reed with the tongue, as this tends to cause a very abrupt cessation of sound.

(*e*) *Inhaling a breath in needless haste.* Obviously there are times when a breath must be taken in very quickly, but try to avoid doing this when it is *not* necessary—for instance, at the beginning of a piece or after a good rest. Do not wait until the last moment, and then hastily gasp in insufficient

[1] Breathing through the nose while actually playing is a method of managing the breath used by some players. I personally do not feel that this is an *essential* part of a fine technical equipment, but its advocates claim that its use makes long phrases and spells of uninterrupted playing easier to manage and less tiring. The method is to keep in the cheeks a reserve of air with which to play, while breathing in and out through the nose. This must be managed with care and taste to prevent the tone sounding uneven and the musical phrasing unpunctuated.

breath just before playing. Having thoroughly exhaled the stale air, breathe in deeply as described on page 5. Then start to play 'on the breath'—that is, as you begin to exhale—feeling the tone flow out as you breathe out firmly and slowly. If you are nervous the steady deep intake of breath will calm you, and make it easier for you to make a clean and controlled start.

(*f*) *Wasting opportunities for breathing.* Because it is easy to play a long phrase without a break, it is often a temptation to try to play *several* long phrases on end without fully using the suitable breathing places, with the result that the cumulative strain begins to tell, and causes uncontrolled playing (and, as I have already said, with beginners, sometimes an uncomfortable feeling of giddiness). Always take every opportunity to breathe out and in as fully as you can: *the importance of this cannot be over-emphasized.* Here are two reminders for 'taking a breath' properly. (i) When exhaling, *push* out the stale air with the abdominal muscles, so that you get rid of as much of it as possible in the time available. (ii) When inhaling, do so completely, using all your breathing muscles.

8. *Vibrato*

The use of vibrato on the oboe has become widely accepted during recent years. Its detractors claim that it destroys the truly characteristic sound of the oboe and prevents its blending well with other instruments in the orchestra. Its advocates feel, I think quite rightly, that a vibrato, *wisely* used, only enhances the natural tone of the instrument. It is my experience that a good vibrato is born and not made: it should come quite naturally, as the student's control develops, so enabling him to express himself musically more fully. Do not *try* to acquire a vibrato without guidance—such efforts so often result in an uncontrolled and most unattractive 'bleating' sound. When a vibrato has started to come naturally, however, it is essential to know how it is being produced, in order to gain real control over it. You should be able to stop it completely at will, and to use it at different degrees of speed (width). It is a good general axiom that you should not have to think about making a vibrato, but about stopping it!

(*a*) *Methods of production.* Vibrato on the oboe is produced by pulsating the air stream used in playing the instrument. There are three ways of doing this: (i) by using the abdominal muscles; (ii) by moving the lips and jaw; (iii) by using the throat muscles.[1]

(i) I is the most satisfactory method, used by the majority of fine players. The abdominal muscles acting on the diaphragm (which is why this method is sometimes called a 'diaphragm vibrato') pulsate the breath as it is being exhaled.[2] Variations in the speed of the vibrato are made by varying the rate of the pulsations. In practice you will find that the wish is really father to the action: when you *want* to slow or quicken your vibrato, your muscles will automatically adjust the speed of the pulsations. Unfortunately it is easy to produce only a very slow pulsation, giving a monotonous wide vibrato; listen to yourself most carefully to avoid this;

(ii) is most inadvisable, for the obvious reason that it is apt to disturb the control of the embouchure. This method should be avoided;

(iii) is a method which can be effective, but it should be used with care—and only by advanced players. Using the throat muscles (rather as you do when making a noise like a nanny goat) is apt to produce too fast a vibrato, by pulsating the air stream too quickly. The player using this method may tend to tighten generally, to force the breath through the reed and to make a good deal of extraneous noise in the throat. The vibrato produced in this way is often hectically fast, very hard to stop or to control; using it may make the player sound consistently nervous, because the tone may be quavery and agitated. Be particularly careful to avoid using a throat vibrato when playing a rapid passage, as it will make the phrase sound uncertain and uneven.

(*b*) *Controlling vibrato.* A good vibrato should liven the tone as the music demands, but using too much vibrato (or too wide a vibrato) may make the oboe player sound like a second-rate violinist playing cheap café music! Remember that most players are apt to use more vibrato than they

---

[1] NEVER try to make a vibrato by moving the oboe, wobbling the fingers, or shaking the head!

[2] To feel this action, appreciably exaggerated, put your hand on your abdomen and say 'Ha-ha-ha' very slowly.

realize. It can very easily be overdone, particularly in the orchestra when you are playing (and should be blending) with other instruments. Vibrato must be used and varied intelligently and musically, and it is vital to practise and to play sometimes *without* it, which at first, you may find difficult. Listen most critically to yourself, and ask your teacher, or someone esle with a reliable musical ear, to tell you whether you *are* playing without vibrato when this is your intention. You may find that when you thought you were playing absolutely without it, you were in fact using just the right amount. It can be used naturally and musically to intensify a crescendo, but beware of using more than your tone will hold, thus producing only a hectic wobbling sound. This is particularly easy if you are using a very soft, free, or close reed, and pushing too much air through it in an attempt to get more sound than it will naturally give. Practise slow scales and long notes daily *without* vibrato. Incidentally this will improve your tone quality and your intonation, for vibrato can cover a multitude of sins.

Try these simple exercises. First, hold a note in an easy register and make a long, slow crescendo, once with vibrato and once without it. Then do the same thing when playing a short series of notes—for instance one octave of a scale. If you have persistent trouble in stopping your vibrato when you wish to, you must persevere with concentrated practice. Spend most of your practice time on scales and exercises without vibrato, and make yourself play less expressively. Always try to relax the throat muscles. Never *push* the breath through the reed; be careful to take in a good deep breath and hold it well back with the abdominal muscles. It may help you to use a reed which has more 'body' in it, i.e. one which vibrates less easily, because the cane is scraped less freely: a thicker reed will not respond quite so sensitively to the smallest variations in the breath stream.

Acquire real control over your vibrato, so that it is your servant and not your master. When you can stop it easily at will, you should play with or without it naturally as the music demands, without any conscious thought or effort.

9. *Nervousness and how to combat it*

Nearly all good players suffer from nervousness, and there is no need to be ashamed of it. In fact, it is often the finest players who suffer most acutely, but naturally, the more control the player has, the less obvious to the listener will be the effects of his nervousness. If you are nervous before playing, you should try to find out for yourself if anything particularly helps you. I do advise eating something before a concert; playing when you have had no food for some hours will usually intensify nervousness. If you are to play a long and exacting solo, try to eat a light but nourishing meal about two hours before it. A little glucose just before the performance is physically invigorating and may be helpful. *However nervous you may feel, never succumb to the temptation of taking alcohol before playing.* 'Dutch courage' will not compensate for lack of control, and it is very dangerous to start a practice which may so easily become a vicious and uncontrollable habit, fatal to fine playing. Most soloists find that a complete rest before a concert is invaluable (if such a thing be possible!), others find that this makes them even more nervous; but you should remember that nervousness is often more acute when you are tired. It is most unwise to work at the piece or passage which is particularly worrying you up to the last moment, thus getting stale. Instead, practise scales and long notes.

The answer to 'nerves' is to acquire more control, and the most important muscles to develop are those which control the breath. If you can manage your breathing when you are nervous, you will find that your embouchure, fingers and tongue are less affected, and that you are steadier generally. When you feel nervous, try these exercises.

(1) A general reviver and 'steadier' for nervousness or tiredness. Stand erect and inhale a full complete breath. While retaining it, extend your arms straight in front of you, letting them feel quite limp and relaxed. Slowly draw your hands back towards your shoulders; gradually contracting the muscles and clenching your fists so that by the time they reach your shoulders your fists will be clenched so tightly that you will feel your arms and hands trembling with the effort. Then,

still holding your breath and keeping the muscles tense, push your fists out slowly and draw them back rapidly. Repeat several times before you drop your arms and exhale vigorously. Then do the exercise on page 8 (once).

(2) To stimulate circulation—particularly helpful if your hands are cold. Stand erect: inhale a full complete breath and retain it. Bend forward slightly and grasp a stick steadily and firmly, gradually exerting your entire strength on the grasp. Relax the grasp, stand upright and exhale slowly. Repeat a few times and finish with the exercise on page 8 (once).

You can use the rail of a chair instead of a stick, and you can easily do this exercise without either—just by exerting your grasp on an imaginary stick.

A 'last-minute' help for nerves is to take a deep breath and hold it for a few seconds before breathing out.

In any problem concerning breath technique try to think of your breathing as punctuation in music. Any breath space you make, however, short and however necessary, should sound as if it were a natural part of the phrase. It should take the place of punctuation in speech: NEVER let it sound like a break made through physical necessity.

EMBOUCHURE CONTROL

The literal translation of the French verb *emboucher* is 'to put in, or to, the mouth', but the noun *embouchure* is used by all wind players in France and in other countries, including Great Britain and the U.S.A., to describe the position of the lips necessary for playing their instrument. The word embouchure thus used implies also the muscular development around the mouthpiece, essential for control. In the case of the oboe, the mouthpiece is the reed.

1. *The functions of the embouchure*

As mentioned briefly at the beginning of Chapter I, the function of the embouchure muscles is to adjust the opening of the reed and so decide the volume of the air stream allowed to go through it, thereby altering the speed, i.e. the *pressure* of the air stream. An air stream of a certain volume going through a small opening will have to go through it more quickly, i.e. at a higher pressure, than the same air stream would go through a larger opening. A simple test without the oboe should make this fact clear to you. Take in a deep breath, and form your lips as if you were going to say an open 'Ah', holding your fingers over your lips, almost touching them. Now breathe out slowly and steadily without varying the volume of the air stream, but as you do so close your lips more—as though you were saying a close 'Oo'. Your fingers should distinctly feel the increase in the speed (pressure) of the air stream as your lips close to shape the 'Oo'.

Therefore, to increase the pressure of the air stream, contract the embouchure muscles to reduce the reed opening. To decrease the pressure of the air stream, relax the embouchure muscles to allow the reed to open.

Obviously the pressure of the air stream will also alter if a varying volume of air is going through an *un*varying opening. Make another simple test to convince yourself of this. Keep your mouth held in a rigid 'Oo' position while you breathe out alternately slowly and quickly; your fingers over your lips

will feel the alterations in the pressure of the air stream as its
volume fluctuates. Always remember then that the breathing
muscles must help the embouchure muscles in their task by
producing the volume of air needed in the circumstances.

A beautiful and *perfectly controlled* tone will only be achieved
when the air stream is managed by the *co-ordinated* control of
the breathing and embouchure muscles.

2. *The formation of the embouchure*

The formation of the embouchure must be guided by the
player's individual physical make-up. To convince yourself
that one good embouchure need not look like another, notice
the wide differences in the formation of the jaws, teeth, lips—
and therefore embouchures—of half a dozen first class oboe
players. But every good embouchure, however formed, should
ultimately achieve a beautiful tone and an accurate and
sensitive control of dynamics and intonation. I shall now
mention briefly some points concerning embouchure forma-
tions, but I must emphasize to beginners that this book should
not be used *instead* of a teacher. When you start playing the
oboe, your embouchure is muscularly quite unformed.
Remember therefore, that until the embouchure muscles are
developed they may feel stiff and uncomfortable, as do any
other muscles when being used much more than usual.[1]

For a time, even if your jaws, teeth, lips, &c., *are* in the
right position, your embouchure may feel uncomfortably
tight and 'gripping'. In the early stages you are incapable
of judging which muscles are working, and it is just as easy
to develop the wrong ones as the right. Such development
is depressingly hard to undo, and I advise you most strongly
to let a good teacher guide you to your natural embouchure,
which must be determined in detail by your own physical
make-up; thus you will avoid developing wrong muscles
and bad habits. Different schools of thought advocate

---

[1] Most advanced players, as well as beginners, suffer at times from dry,
chapped, or sore lips. I find, as do many other wind players, that camphor
ice ointment is most efficacious for relieving these conditions. Should the
lips get sore *inside*, where they roll over the teeth, surgical spirit dabbed on
the spot will be helpful. The cause of this may be over-playing (particularly
if you are a beginner), using too open or too strong a reed, keeping the teeth
too close together and/or pressing the lips hard on the teeth.

C

different methods of control which involve using certain muscles to a greater or lesser degree, different types of reeds, varying positions for the jaws, teeth, lips, tongue, &c. There is no space here for me to enumerate the pros and cons of the differing ways of playing. In any case such a procedure might well be most misleading since, as I have already said, an embouchure must be of necessity an individual thing. I shall however describe two very different general *types* of embouchure.

The first I shall call the '*tight*' *embouchure*, and at the risk of being controversial, I consider it one to be most strenuously avoided. The teeth are close together, the lips stretched tightly over them, and the reed is pressed between the lips as if in a clamp with a fairly strong 'bite'. Control comes mainly from the muscles at the corners of the mouth, which stretch the lips more or less tightly over the teeth. The other I shall call a '*flexible*' *embouchure*, and since it is the one I personally advocate, I shall describe it in more detail.

To form this type of embouchure, the upper and lower jaws and teeth are held firmly quite well apart to make a resilient framework to support the lips, thus allowing the lips themselves to act as springy muscular 'cushions' for the reed, holding it not in a rigid, pinching grip but with a gentle firmness, allowing the breath to go freely through it, and the opening of the reed to be easily and *minutely* adjusted. NEVER clamp the reed tightly between the lips and teeth, forcing the breath through it with the throat muscles. Try to think of a free stream of air flowing from the base of your chest (its volume graduated by the breathing muscles) through the throat and reed and right down the oboe, controlled on its way by the springy firmness of the embouchure. Your throat muscles should never be tight and rigid.

If you are a beginner, you will probably find it extremely difficult to relax the muscles of your embouchure and throat; you may tend to pinch the reed tightly, sometimes even shutting it up altogether so that no sound comes. Often the harder you *try* to relax the more you will tighten, because you are so conscious of that particular part of your body. A good way to relax in one part is to tighten in another, and since the diaphragm and the abdominal wall should really be taut when you play, try consciously contracting them, feeling them hard and springy, while standing up straight and pulling in your lower abdomen.

It must be remembered, however, that the opening of the reed is very small, and that the muscles of the embouchure must hold it firmly *enough* (*a*) to allow the pressure of the breath to make the reed vibrate; (*b*) to control the variations in the air stream going through it, and (*c*) to prevent any air from escaping around it. But let me remind you again that this grip must always be a firm yet springy and flexible one all round the reed—never a tight, pinching clamp between the lips pulled rigidly over the teeth. Try to think almost of O rather than of E.

3. *General advice for a flexible embouchure*

(*a*) The lower jaw should be pulled slightly down and back, the teeth fairly well apart. This 'framework' for the lips should stay firm as you play.

(*b*) The lips should be rolled over the teeth and drawn in as if by a rubber band in the middle, forming springy muscular cushions to hold and control the reed. NEVER let the reed come directly in contact with the teeth.

(*c*) The muscles round the lips should be firm; not rigid.

(*d*) Do not pinch the reed tightly between the lips, but never let air escape from around the reed, nor allow bulges of air anywhere. These bulges often occur between the lips and teeth, or in the cheeks, and they are a sign that there is a lack of muscular control from the lips around the reed. They may affect the tone and control adversely by wasting breath pressure and disturbing the embouchure.[1] Practise in front of a looking-glass, and if you see or feel these air bulges forming, stop playing and start again with a fresh embouchure. If you find that this failing is hard to overcome, try using a softer reed, and avoid playing when your embouchure feels tired.

[1] A further reason why these air bulges should be avoided is because the air in the cheeks can be forced into the duct of the parotid gland, thus causing considerable discomfort. (The parotid gland makes the saliva pass its secretions through the duct into the mouth.) Should this happen, the discomfort can be speedily relieved by massaging the middle of the cheek, from behind forward.

(*e*) Learn to feel the right amount of reed in your mouth, and judge this by the quality of sound you are producing (see later, in section 6 *b*). The correct amount of reed in the mouth, i.e. the amount covered by the lips, must vary slightly according to the embouchure and the type of reed used, and it must also be sensitively adjusted by the player in order to control dynamics and intonation. Generally speaking, the more contracted the embouchure the more of the reed should be covered by the lips, so that they may control it more firmly. I must emphasize that these alterations to the position of the reed in the mouth are *minute*, and more often than not they can only be felt and not seen. Do not pull the oboe away from the embouchure nor push towards it as you play, thus *radically* altering the position of the reed in the mouth. Always hold the instrument steadily in its normal position.

(*f*) *The angle at which the oboe is held* is of vital importance to the correct formation of the embouchure. As a general rule, there should not be an uneven pressure from the lips on the two blades of the reed, for this would affect its vibration and thus cause resistance to the air column flowing through the instrument. Therefore, again as a general rule, one lip should not protrude appreciably beyond the other. In many embouchures, the formation of the teeth and/or the comparative shortness of the upper lip make it necessary for the upper jaw, and therefore lip, to jut out slightly over the lower. In my experience however, it is very rarely necessary for the lower jaw to protrude beyond the upper. As a guide, the average angle for holding the oboe is at 45 degrees from the body, but you must determine for yourself the angle at which your embouchure is comfortable and right.

If you hold your oboe at too *wide* an angle from the body, by lifting it too high while letting your head drop, you will take the reed away from the framework of the lower jaw and the cushion of the lower lip, causing the upper lip to press too hard. This will often cause a general flatness of pitch, particularly of the upper notes, and a dead, unresonant sound. Keep your chin in and your neck straight, not bent over.

If you hold your oboe at too *acute* an angle from the body, by dropping it too low while keeping your head up, you will support the reed too much on the lower lip and teeth, and the upper lip will be stretched too tightly to give the necessary cushioned control. This will often cause a general sharpness of pitch, particularly of the upper notes, and a hard sound.

Practising with mirrors so that you can see your profile is helpful for correcting faults of posture and of embouchure (and incidentally for avoiding affected and exaggerated movements) but you should very soon be able to *feel* when the position of your oboe and your embouchure is correct, guided by the quality of the sound you are producing.

4. *Pitch*

The correct pitch today is $A = 440$. Test the pitch of your oboe by blowing your lower A steadily and comparing it with that of the requisite tuning-fork. (Pianos vary appreciably in pitch, and are therefore unreliable as a guide.) If your pitch is not correct, there may be several reasons to account for this. If you are *very* sharp (a quarter of a tone or more) you may have a sharp pitch oboe, and in this case you should consult a professional player or a reliable instrument-maker. You may flatten the pitch a very little by slightly pulling the reed out of the instrument, but more than a tiny amount will affect the general intonation of your oboe, as it will flatten some notes out of proportion to the rest. The instrument will also be less responsive, because pulling out the staple distorts the bore at that point. If you are consistently flat, your oboe may have been built to the flatter pitch of $A = 435$ (this applies to many older instruments) and you can use staples and reeds to counteract this—in consultation with an expert. Remember that temperature will affect the pitch, so bear this in mind when testing it. The oboe will play flatter when it is cold; sharper when it is well warmed. Other troubles with the general pitch may be due (*a*) to staples of the wrong length or bore, and/or a wrongly made reed, or (*b*) to a faulty embouchure.

(*a*) These points will be discussed in Chapter 6.

(*b*) The general pitch will incline to be *sharp* if:
    the embouchure is gripping the reed too tightly,
    the lips are rolled too far over the teeth,
    the reed is too far in the mouth.

The general pitch will incline to be *flat* if:
> the embouchure is not holding the reed firmly enough,
> the lips are not rolled far enough over the teeth,
> the reed is not far enough in the mouth.

Also, as I have already said, a faulty embouchure caused by holding the oboe incorrectly can affect the general pitch and intonation.

5. *Intonation and dynamics*

Fine intonation is vital on any instrument, but since the natural quality of the oboe tone is so concentrated and clearly defined, imperfect intonation on the oboe sounds particularly painful, and you must guard against it with all possible care. Playing well in tune depends on the ear's ability to judge the correct intonation of each note, and on the control of the muscles necessary to adjust the pitch according to the ear's dictates. Some players are born with a better musical ear than others, but any musical ear—even a poor one—can be improved by concentrated practice. Always listen to yourself with the most critical attention, for playing out of tune can so easily become a careless habit which spoils the performance even of accomplished players. Vibrato can camouflage this fault, so practise slow scales and long notes *without* it. Try always to hear the note you are going to play before you actually play it: this should very soon become automatic, even when sight-reading.

As I have explained, the control of intonation and dynamics is achieved by *slight* alterations to the volume and pressure of the air stream, and these alterations are managed by the *co-ordinated* actions of the breathing muscles and the embouchure muscles. Always bear in mind this fundamental principle, particularly as you read the rest of this chapter.

The following points are generalizations, and like those given earlier they may not apply to all situations with all types of embouchure. They are given as sign-posts by which the player may find the way more easily to the ultimate goal, which should be sensitive and automatic control without any conscious thought of what the muscles are actually doing.

(*a*) *Notes in varying registers.* As a broad generalization, the higher the note the higher the pressure of the air stream—

the firmer the embouchure and the farther the lips roll over the teeth, thus covering more of the reed. The opposite also applies. The lower the note the lower the pressure of the air stream—the more relaxed the embouchure and the less the lips are rolled over the teeth, thus covering less of the reed.

(*b*) *Tuning.*

To sharpen: contract the embouchure.

To flatten: relax the embouchure.

There are very few oboes in existence—if any!—which do not have at least one or two slightly faulty notes, and these will have to be 'humoured' by the embouchure to be perfectly in tune. But *all* embouchure adjustments are so very sensitive and small that if you listen carefully to your intonation, your muscles will soon learn to adjust the embouchure automatically without any conscious thought on your part.

(*c*) *Crescendo and diminuendo.*

To make a crescendo:

(1) Breathe out more quickly, i.e. increase the volume of the air stream. The air should flow freely up from the chest. Do not use the throat muscles to check it, and then force it on through the reed.

(2) The reed must be allowed to open gradually in order to admit the increasing stream of air. Relax the embouchure, allowing the lips to roll less over the teeth. A tendency to sharpen the pitch during a crescendo may be due to the embouchure not relaxing sufficiently and/or too much of the reed being covered by the lips.

To make a diminuendo:

(1) Breathe out more slowly, i.e. decrease the volume of the air stream. Let the reduced air stream flow gently and freely. The abdominal muscles should hold it back; do not check it with your throat muscles.

(2) The opening of the reed must become gradually closer. Contract the embouchure, rolling the lips farther over the teeth. A tendency to flatten during a diminuendo may be due to the embouchure not contracting enough and/or the reed not being covered sufficiently by the lips.

It is particularly difficult to play piano in the lower register and to play forte on the upper notes with a fine

sound and intonation. Both these procedures require the very
sensitive and co-ordinated control of the breathing and
embouchure muscles which can only be achieved after long
practice. As I have repeatedly emphasized, the embouchure
is an individual and sensitive thing. It would therefore be
dangerously misleading for me to attempt to describe the exact
muscular actions involved in relaxing or contracting it. You
will very soon learn to feel such processes for yourself. *All*
embouchure control must come mainly from the lips themselves, and from the muscles supporting them. There is no
need whatsoever for any larger movement—of the jaws or
the head, for instance—nor should the oboe be pulled in and
out to alter the amount of reed in the mouth.

*At all times, the tone should sound free, and in tune—whether
loud or soft—anywhere on the instrument, with a cantabile legato over
all intervals.* This ideal will only be achieved when the breathing muscles can accurately control the volume of the air
stream and the embouchure muscles can exactly adjust the
opening of the reed to accommodate the air stream going
through it.[1] This means that the muscles of breathing and
of the embouchure must be developed so that they can be
controlled to a most sensitive degree, and this co-ordinated
control can most speedily be acquired by regular and frequent
practice of very slow legato scales, in all keys, played thus:

(The breathing place is marked V. Beginners should breathe
at the marks VV.)

[1] *The Oboe Tutor* written in the early nineteenth century by Sellner is
rather out of date today, but in his long-winded sentences he gives some sound
advice. He says: 'The pressure of the lips should never be stronger than is de-
manded for introducing as much air into the reed as is needed for producing
the sound it is desired to make, since the greater and the more free the resonance of the notes, the easier it will be found to succeed in playing the
instrument in general. In short, the whole study of the oboe should have
the end of acquiring that true skill which enables the sound, or voice, of the
instrument to be produced with only the lightest necessary hold on the reed
and without any roughness or dissonance. This art cannot be obtained
without an intelligent teacher and much practice.'

Develop the muscles also by embouchure exercises—for instance, the following. Starting on the low F, play thus on each note, chromatically up to the F above. As you gain control extend the exercise down to the bottom B flat and up to the F in the third register. (The same applies to all similar exercises.)

Practise this on all notes:

Work at octaves thus on all notes up the scale

&c.,

then down

Then:

and so on chromatically as far as the top F. Then down:

Practise these octave exercises first playing steadily mezzo forte, then piano, and finally with the dynamics as marked.

6. *Tone quality*

A beautiful tone is the greatest asset of any oboe player. Always listen to the sound you are making and be critical of its quality, for the *wish* to make a lovely sound is really father to the producing of it. A poor tone quality may be caused by—

(*a*) a faulty breath control,
(*b*) a wrong embouchure,
(*c*) a bad or unsuitable reed;

or by a combination of these.

(*a*) Wrong control of the volume of the air stream with the throat muscles may make the tone uneven, and sometimes 'loose' and over-vibrant. Not taking in enough breath, i.e. not having a high enough air pressure available, may produce a dead, unresonant quality of sound. If you try to push too much breath through the reed you will make a coarse and uncontrolled sound generally known as 'overblowing', and unexpected squawks may occur on some notes! Using too little breath to make the reed vibrate properly will not 'fill' the instrument. The tone will be thin and spasmodic, and certain notes—particularly the bottom ones—may not sound at all. To use the wind-player's expression, they may not 'speak'.

(*b*) A bad tone may be caused by a faulty embouchure in different ways, usually by gripping too much with the upper or lower lip or both, and often by having a faulty support for the lips (the lower or upper jaw too far protruded, the teeth too far or not far enough apart, the muscles round the mouth too tightly contracted or too slack, &c.).

Let me advise you once more to seek advice on forming— or altering—your embouchure from someone who is really qualified to help you.

The right amount of reed covered by the lips must vary according to the player and his physical formation, the reed used, and the circumstances. To say that about one-third to one-half of the cane should be covered is but to give the beginner a rough idea, and as I have said it is only by experi- ence that you will find exactly the right place for the reed in

the mouth by the 'feel' of it, after listening carefully to the
sound you make during your early stages. If you have too
much reed in the mouth, the tone will sound loud, coarse,
thick and 'woody' and will incline to be sharp in pitch: if
you have too little, the sound will be small, squeezed, thin,
and 'reedy' or 'tinny' and inclined to be flat, particularly on
the top notes.

(c) Tone quality can be affected by the reed: this will be
discussed briefly in Chapter VI.

A fine, well controlled tone and intonation is a far greater
asset than a very rapid staccato and quickly moving fingers.
Obviously, a first-class player should have *all* these qualities;
but the student's first aim should be to play a slow tune
beautifully. Never try to run about the instrument while
practising before you have learned to 'walk' with real control.
At the same time, remember that untidy fingers can spoil
your tone and musical line. The temptation to go on playing
slow tunes you can manage easily, instead of working at finger
and tongue control, must be resisted just as strongly as the
temptation to rush about the instrument without being critical
of your tone and intonation.

III

TONGUE CONTROL

1. *The action of the tongue*

The tongue must *always* be used when beginning a phrase[1] to start the reed vibrating, and also for punctuating the air stream to make detached sounds of varying lengths. To 'tongue' a note say 'Ter' with your tongue on the reed. As you normally say 'Ter' the tip of your tongue gently hits the roof of your mouth just above your front teeth, and quickly springs away again. Exactly the same thing happens when you say 'Ter' with the oboe, except that the tip of your tongue hits the tip of the *reed*, and springs away again. The action of the tongue should be quite gentle: in a detached passage, it is merely to punctuate the air stream by stopping the vibration of the reed for a tiny fraction of a second. Try to feel as if the air stream were going through the oboe continuously while you are playing a detached phrase; think of such a passage as a punctuated legato line, rather than as a series of separate notes.

2. *Varying the length of staccato and the type of attack*

The length of the detached notes may be varied by the consonant pronounced by the tongue on the reed. Ter will produce a short sound and Der a longer and gentler one, and all variations in the length of detached notes and types of attack may be obtained by pronouncing these Ter and Der sounds slightly differently according to requirements. (A *very* soft and gentle attack, or a melodic, singing type of detached note, may be made with the tongue rather relaxed, touching the reed with a stroking movement: but this method should not be attempted until a real control of the embouchure has been achieved.) The tongue should never be tight and rigid, however short the staccato. Beginners may find that the movements of the tongue may tend to disturb the

---

[1] Modern composers may require the player to start notes without tonguing, using only the breath. This is seldom necessary, and NEVER to be attempted by beginners.

embouchure and perhaps unfurl the lips from over the teeth, causing air to leak from around the reed. Therefore their natural instinct while tonguing is to tighten the embouchure in the effort to control it. When the tongue movements are properly graduated this tightening of the embouchure will not normally be found necessary, because the correct movements of the tongue should be too slight to disturb the embouchure. Until this control has been acquired, try consciously to relax your embouchure—as well as the tongue itself—when you practise tonguing, in order to counteract the instinctive tendency to tighten needlessly. For a real forte-piano, which necessitates a very sharp attack from the tongue accompanied by a sudden momentary increase of breath, the muscles of the embouchure must relax and contract again instantaneously. On the comparatively rare occasions when you want the shortest possible sound, or when the end of a phrase must be stopped very abruptly, the tongue should touch the reed and spring away as usual, and then *immediately* come back on to the reed again to stop it vibrating, almost as if you were saying 'Tut' very sharply.

3. *Practising tongue control*

Start exercising the tongue without moving the fingers by holding a note, first in an easy register and then anywhere on the instrument, punctuating the sound with the tongue. Begin simply by saying Ter several times, then Der, and later try to vary the lengths of these consonants to make different types of detached sounds. Then play scales, slowly at first, repeating each note four times, then each note three times, then each note twice. Finally play the scales tonguing each note, gradually increasing the speed as the muscles of the tongue and fingers learn to work together. This scale exercise can be practised using varying lengths of staccato. Later, practise scales in thirds in the same way; then exercises and studies to acquire the harder synchronization of tongue and fingers in the wider, and varied intervals.

Practise tonguing frequently with the metronome. To increase the speed of your tongue when you are past the beginning stage, play a staccato scale as fast as you can. Then set the metronome a little faster, and try again. The incentive of the relentless metronome beat will often make you realize that you *can* tongue more quickly than you thought you could! When practising in this way it is essential to remember that the notes must be clean and even. It is a waste of time to increase the speed untidily and unevenly. Bear in mind that a reed with too much resistance can make speedy tonguing more difficult. Try to acquire a classic, melodic staccato with real tone in each note. Think legato as you play staccato.

4. *Double, triple, and flutter tonguing*

Double tonguing is produced by pronouncing two syllables alternately, Ter-Ker. The Ter is the usual way with the tongue on the reed, and the Ker just as when spoken. This method of tonguing is effectively used on some other wind instruments (notably the flute) but it is less satisfactory on the oboe because of the difficulty of making the Ker sound as clean and sharp as the Ter, particularly when playing wider intervals. It is also hard to control the speed of double tonguing on the oboe.

Some players use it extensively and successfully. Personally I agree with the many others who consider it wiser and more satisfactory to practise to quicken their single tonguing, reserving the use of double for the rare occasions when the speed of good single tonguing is really inadequate. Triple tonguing is akin to double; it is achieved by saying Ter-Ker-Ter or Ter-Ter-Ker, or Ter-Ker-Ter/Ker-Ter-Ker alternately.

Flutter tonguing is impracticable on the oboe—though composers have been known to ask for it! It is produced by rolling an R while playing, with a relaxed embouchure and very little reed in the mouth.

Tonguing is the equivalent of bowing on a stringed instrument. When you have real tongue control, be guided by your sense of style and musicianship to use it in the fullest possible way, as a fine string player uses the bow.

IV

FINGER CONTROL

1. How to hold the oboe and use the fingers

The oboe should be held so that the reed is quite steady in the embouchure while the fingers and left thumb may move freely and comfortably. Stand or sit as described in Chapter I, with the elbows raised and held away from the sides without any stiffness, the backs of the hands in an almost straight line with the wrists and elbows. The instrument is designed to balance easily on the right thumb and a little practice will make this balance simple and natural. (A thin layer of cork or thick felt glued under the thumb-rest may make it more comfortable for the right thumb.)

The length of the fingers and the shape of the hand must determine how far the thumb is placed under the thumb-rest—normally not more than the top joint. If the thumb is too far under its rest, the right-hand fingers will be very cramped; they should lie and move easily on the oboe. The pads of the fingers should be nearly flat on the holes or keys, and the fingers will usually move more easily and comfortably if they are not too bent at the joints.

The left thumb should normally be on the thumb-plate (or if you use the Conservatoire system, on the instrument just below the octave key or keys). It should be placed flat and very near the octave key, so that it can roll over on to it. Do not move the whole thumb on and off—use the left side of it with a rotary action; a very slight pressure is enough to work the octave key. The second octave key should also be worked with a rotary movement (a very small one from the left wrist), the left elbow well up and the wrist flat to allow freedom for this. The first three fingers on each hand should move freely but firmly up and down, with enough strength to close the hole or press the key concerned. Some players find it easier to control their fingers if they lift them higher and bring them down harder, but any *very* strong pressure or violent action may tend to shake the oboe and so affect the embouchure. Let the fingers move with a fairly flat action, so that their pads can cover the hole or plate or move the key. When at rest, the finger pads should remain as close as possible to the ring or key they work.

2. *Training the muscles*

It is vital to train the fingers and left thumb to cover holes, &c., at an even speed. Sometimes students who are particularly gifted musically acquire comparatively early a lovely and controlled tone, but do not seem able to discipline their fingers equally well. This may be because they do not practise this branch of technique in the right way. Finger practice is a matter of mind over muscles, and much of it is also a matter of mind over musical feelings. In order to make the notes sound absolutely clean and *even* at all speeds, which is the essence of finger control, it is often necessary when practising to force yourself *not* to shape a phrase musically, but to play it evenly—mechanically note by note. When your fingers are really disciplined, you can then phrase as you wish, untrammelled by any unintentional unevenness. Never allow yourself to play a phrase freely until you can play it accurately in strict time. A passage can so often be made easier for the fingers by using rubato, but beware of the danger of doing this just because it *is* easier. Never allow your fingers to play a phrase their way.

The best way to acquire finger control is to practise scales and exercises, starting with those in the easier keys. Start very slowly and increase the speed only gradually, always playing rhythmically and evenly. Use your brain, and *think* and hear evenly; do not let the slightest unevenness pass— *at any speed*. Practise all scales and exercises in varying rhythms and articulations, and make exercises for yourself to develop weak or sluggish fingers, or to perfect the difficult parts of any scale or passage. Uncontrolled fingers will cause interpolated notes to sound in slow practising; scales in thirds are particularly valuable for checking such untidiness, and for training the lips and fingers to act well together. Remember that however slowly you are moving from note to note, your fingers must react quickly; but the more slowly you practise, the more quickly will your fingers learn control.

3. *Good and bad habits*

Tables of fingering are obtainable in tutors and methods.[1]
These tables give the usual and often alternative ways of
producing each note. If there is an alternative fingering,
always use the one which produces the best sound and intonation, and resist the temptation to use the sometimes easier but
poorer-sounding fake fingerings; for instance, the open C
sharp. Fake fingerings, such as trill keys, leaving unnecessary
fingers down, or unorthodox keys open or shut, should be
used only by players who are advanced enough to judge
whether the difficulty or speed of a passage justifies their use.

Try to avoid such common faults as these:

(a) Keeping the D sharp key open while playing E.

(b) Opening the E flat key for a forked F which is already
adequately vented mechanically, or *not* using that key if
an *un*vented forked F is really improved by it.

(c) Sliding untidily from C sharp to D sharp with the
right-hand little finger, instead of acquiring the good
habit of using the alternative left-hand D sharp key.

(d) Slovenly changes of fingers between the B flat and B
natural, in all registers.

(e) Using the wrong octave key. Unless you have automatic octave keys, you must play E to G sharp inclusive
with the first octave key, and A to C inclusive with the
second. The C sharp, D, and D sharp in the second
register are produced by taking off the first finger of the
left hand (or on certain instruments by rolling it over on
to the plate), NOT by using either octave key.

When it is necessary to slide a finger over keys, for instance
bottom B flat to B natural or C to C sharp, you may find it
easier to use the flat of the finger tip, without bending the
joint. To facilitate sliding, *slightly* grease the finger concerned.
(An old professional trick is to rub it in the hair or at the side
of the nose!) For the C sharp and D trill keys played with
the right-hand second finger and with the left-hand second
and third fingers, most players find it easier to strike the key

[1] An elementary one is given in the *Otto Langey Tutor*, pub. Boosey &
Hawkes, and a very comprehensive one for the Conservatoire system in
Gillet's *Studies for the Advanced Teaching of the Oboe*, pub. Leduc.

D

with the flat part of the finger below the first joint, rather than with its tip. For slurring between bottom B and G sharp, or between D sharp and G sharp, it is often easier to put the fourth finger of the left hand on *both* the keys concerned. (These shifts are simpler on an oboe having an alternative G sharp key.)

4. *Harmonics and high notes*

(*a*) *Harmonics.* Certain harmonics may be played on some instruments (not all of them on those with fully automatic, i.e. double acting, octaves) and can be extremely useful.

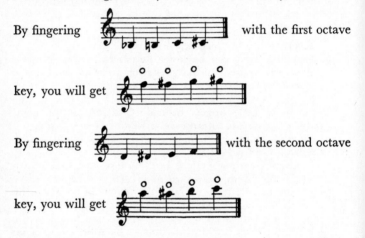

By fingering [score] with the first octave

key, you will get [score]

By fingering [score] with the second octave

key, you will get [score]

These notes played as harmonics have quite a different quality of tone—a much less resonant and vibrant sound—than when they are fingered normally. The harmonics can be very useful for tone colour effects in solo playing, as well as in the orchestra when a quiet, unobtrusive sound is needed. Their notes are inclined to be flat in pitch, and they need to be blown rather more strongly than when fingered normally to produce approximately the same volume of piano sound. (They are no use for forte playing.) These qualities make them useful for playing pianissimo notes which might otherwise tend to be sharp and/or hard to control, through nerves, a difficult reed, &c., &c.

(*b*) *High notes.* For the notes above C in the third register no octave key is used on many instruments.[1] The embouchure for the E and onwards is appreciably more contracted than in the lower registers. As a general rule, the lips tighten and roll over farther, thus covering more of the reed (in the majority of embouchures the lower lip particularly is concerned in this action) and more support is given from the muscles at the corners of the mouth. I would advise beginners not to try to play above C until their embouchure is fairly comfortable elsewhere. When the muscles are developed, most of these top notes will come quite easily and the embouchure will adjust for them naturally, without the forceful gripping an unformed embouchure would have to make. For more advanced players I would advocate practising in the register normally used in the oboe repertoire (up to the top F sharp or G). It is a waste of practice time to expend energy trying to play notes of mainly academic interest. For the notes in the third register there are often variations of fingerings, particularly on instruments without the automatic octave keys. Once your embouchure and finger control is sufficiently assured to be certain of the high notes with the fingerings you normally use, you should experiment with variations. Often the pitch and quality of a note can be varied to suit different instruments, reeds, or circumstances. Here is an example:

The most usual fingering for the C sharp in the third register on the thumb-plate system is:

Left hand: Second and third fingers down (and thumb-plate).
Right hand: First and third fingers down, plus the C sharp key.

Now, leaving the left-hand fingers in the same position, try altering the right-hand finger positions in these three ways, by using (*a*) only the first finger, (*b*) the first finger and also the low C natural key, (*c*) the first and third fingers with the low C natural key. You will find that these variations in fingering may produce differences in the sound and pitch of the top C sharp.

Alternative fingerings for notes in the third register vary

[1] Others have a third octave key for the highest register.

according to the instrument, its system and its adjustment. Learn the various fingerings which suit your own oboe and reeds and then use them wisely as the occasion demands. Remember that fingering some top notes with only the left hand can be convenient, particularly in rapid passage work, but on most instruments the top notes produced in this way tend to be less stable in pitch, and to require more sensitive embouchure control. Beginners should learn the fingerings involving also the use of the right hand, and use only these until a fairly good embouchure control has been acquired.

V

THE INSTRUMENT AND ITS CARE

1. *Choice of system and keywork*

There are two general systems of fingering,[1] and the vital differences between them concern only the notes in the middle of the instrument; the B flat to C natural inclusive, in the second and third registers. In the thumb-plate system, which is the one more often used in Great Britain, the left-hand thumb, or right-hand side key, is used in fingering these notes. In the Conservatoire system, used very widely in Europe and in the U.S.A., the first three fingers of the right hand work the necessary mechanism. There is really little to choose between the two systems. The thumb-plate system may make the middle B flat sound a little bright in comparison with the rest of the instrument; with the Conservatoire system it often has a rather rounder and less resonant sound. On the other hand, the middle C is usually a fuller and better note on the thumb-plate system. In either case a skilled player can minimize the change of tone quality, and from the angle of fingering there is again little to choose: different passages may be easier or harder on one system than on the other. Octave keys may be fully automatic (double-acting), semi-automatic, or simple (single-acting). I would recommend either of the second two systems. The fully automatic system may make the fingering of certain passages slightly simpler but it has the serious disadvantages of often giving trouble mechanically, of making the extreme top notes more difficult to play—by limiting the variations of fingerings for them—and the use of some harmonics impossible. You can have an oboe with covered holes, known sometimes as the plateaux system. These instruments are built with flat discs covering all holes (like a flute), instead of having open rings on some of them. The advantage of the system is that the fingers need not be

[1] Other systems are: (*a*) the old German system, still widely used in Germany—mainly by older players and by beginners using old second-hand instruments. It involves the use of right-hand side keys for the B flat and C. (*b*) The highly individual system, used almost exclusively in Vienna, which preserves some of the features of the eighteenth-century oboe.

placed quite so carefully, thus facilitating rapid passage work: the disadvantage is that the mechanism is more complicated, and more liable to get out of order and to need constant attention in order to work perfectly. This system slightly alters the tone quality of the instrument, making it a little less bright and vibrant—'darker' in sound.

Extra keys may be added or incorporated, such as the long F, long C sharp, side G sharp, third octave key, and various couplings, trill keys, &c. Their use is mainly a matter of habit, and they are not essential. If you have too elaborate a system of keywork, you run the risk of making the oboe uncomfortably weighty to hold, and liable to need constant mechanical attention. It is usually better to practise until you have perfected simple fingerings with your existing keywork, rather than to have a special key put on your instrument in order to cover an awkward shift or trill! Of all the 'extras', the ones generally considered most useful are the long F (particularly if the forked F is not a good one), the long C sharp, and the side G sharp. A coupling which causes the low B flat and B natural keys automatically to hold down the low C natural key is most useful, and is neither a heavy nor a complicated piece of mechanism. An alternative is a coupling between the B and C sharp keys. In my opinion the advantages of the former coupling outweigh its disadvantage of making certain alternative fingerings impossible in the high register.

2. *The care of the oboe*

For technical proficiency your oboe must be in good mechanical order. Always remember that it is a delicately adjusted instrument, and that it will serve you more reliably if it is given the occasional attention which all fine mechanism needs and deserves. *Try to avoid subjecting it to violent extremes and exaggerated changes of temperature, or to excessive jolting or vibration.*

(*a*) *Cleaning.* Your warm breath going through the oboe will cause condensation in the bore (the inside), particularly when the instrument is cold, and this moisture must be removed before putting the oboe away. Use a large feather from the tail of a cock pheasant or a turkey, or a pull-through cleaner made of fine material sewn to a weight small enough to pass through the top joint. Avoid using mops and brushes; they tend to shed fibres which may get under the pads, and when worn, the wire support can scratch the bore. Be sure that the very top of the bore is clean: if it gets slightly blocked with dirt, fluff, &c., the top notes may be flat. If a hole gets water in it, first clean the bore and then put a piece of cigarette paper on the hole to absorb the water. (Avoid using the paper's gummed edge.) Blowing sharply across the hole will often get rid of some water, and make it easier to mop up the rest under the pad. Persistent trouble with water under a pad may be caused by the grain of the wood or dirt or roughness in the bore making the water run in a particular direction. An oily feather passed through the bore may cure this tendency: if not, consult a qualified repairer or maker.

Water in the tiny hole of either octave key may cause the upper notes to drop an octave, and to clean an octave key properly takes a little more time. First take the instrument to pieces and clean the bore. Hold the top joint, and put cigarette paper under the octave hole which is giving trouble. Cover the holes of the top joint with the left-hand fingers as you would for fingering G, and completely close the end of the joint with your right-hand fingers. Now blow through the top of the joint while opening and shutting the octave key concerned, and then mop up the moisture under the pad with fresh cigarette papers. This is often caused by playing on a cold instrument, but if it occurs frequently, take the oboe to a reliable repairer who will take out the key and 'cup' and clean the hole thoroughly.

Never polish the keywork: there is always the danger of (i) getting polishing material under the pads and (ii) rubbing vigorously enough to bend or misplace the delicate and finely adjusted mechanism. When you have finished playing, just wipe the keywork gently with a chamois leather. Be particularly careful to do this if your hands are inclined to perspire. About once a month you can dust lightly around the keywork with a small dry paintbrush, brushing the dust away from the holes and pads. Never disturb the mechanism without due reason. Slight adjustments may be necessary from time to time, particularly on a new oboe, or on one recently overhauled—until the pads have 'settled'. It is useful to be able to make these adjustments yourself but rather than risk damage, go to an expert. Always keep your oboe in a properly fitted case when not in use. If you do put it down for a few moments without cleaning it or taking it apart, always incline it on the left-hand feather keys (i.e. the bottom B flat and B natural keys), so that any water in the bore will run away from the holes. When 'resting', never hold the oboe with the holes or the top of it downwards.

(*b*) *Greasing*. The cork joints should be greased occasionally, so that they slide easily into the sockets, thus avoiding the danger of damaging the keywork by forcing the joints together. First clean the cork with spirit and then work a little grease such as vaseline into it. Should the corks become too slack they may need renewing, but as an emergency measure clean them well with spirit, then wet them thoroughly and warm them carefully with a lighted match or taper. This will cause the cork to swell slightly. Staples which are too slack or too stiff in the socket may be treated in the same way. A slack staple may also be made to fit more tightly by wrapping cigarette paper round the cork.

(*c*) *Oiling*. The mechanism should be oiled with clock oil three or four times a year, and even more frequently if necessary in certain climates. Apply just a drop with a needle on every moving joint, and then move the keywork concerned to let the oil work in. It is a good plan also to oil the springs, which may otherwise tend to rust, using a little oil on a pipe-cleaner. Incidentally, an emergency substitute for a spring can often be made with an elastic band: it is a good plan to keep a few small ones handy. Always be very careful not to let any oil get under the pads: it is a wise precaution to put cigarette papers under them while you are oiling. If a *dry* pad sticks, dust it with French chalk. As an alternative, take a piece of stiff paper which has been well blackened with a soft lead pencil; hold the paper firmly against the pad while pulling it slowly away.

Reputable instrument-makers, and also players, disagree about the advisability of oiling the wood of the oboe. Some believe that regularly oiling the bore preserves the wood, and helps to prevent cracks in it which might be caused by its being insufficiently matured, by extreme climates, or by violent changes of temperature. Others hold that the wood normally used today (grenadilla or African blackwood) is too hard and non-absorbent for oiling to affect it. If you do oil the bore of your oboe, possibly on the considered advice of your teacher or instrument-maker or repairer, use a feather dipped in the oil (almond is suitable), but remove all excess oil from the feather with your fingers before putting it through the bore lest you get oil through the holes and under the pads.

(d) *Precautions in extreme temperatures.* On occasions when you must take the oboe from a particularly hot or cold temperature outside to play in a well-heated or air-cooled building, put the instrument together and leave it (for 15–30 minutes if possible) before playing on it. If the oboe has to be kept in an over-heated or overcooled room (which is inadvisable), put it in a cupboard or drawer and away from radiators or fans.

I strongly advise the regular use of a waterproof cover for your oboe case when carrying it out of doors, as a protection against extremes of temperature and humidity.

Finally, at least every few years take the oboe to a reputable maker or repairer for an overhaul: otherwise it may give you trouble at an unexpected and inopportune moment.

VI

REEDS AND THEIR CARE

More than one well-known oboe player has been known to say that the reed accounts for at least 80 per cent. of the oboist's troubles, or success! Be this as it may, all oboe players find technical problems easier on a reed which entirely suits them, and it is therefore essential to consider the choice and care of reeds as a technical problem in itself. To go into the whole science and art of reed-making in all its stages would need the space of a book and in this chapter I shall only attempt to give the briefest outline of the process, and a collection of hints which may be helpful to reed-makers and reed-scrapers.

1. *The importance of the staple*[1]

The staple is a tube of metal, partly covered with cork, which supports the cane. This tube is conically bored, and it should be scientifically made to play in tune when pushed right home into the socket. As I have said earlier, it is possible to flatten the general pitch slightly by pulling out the staple a little, but this will flatten some notes out of proportion to others, and will also tend to make the instrument less responsive, because of this slight distortion to its bore. Staples may vary in metal, thickness, bore, and length, and can cause differences in pitch, intonation, and reed opening. You may find that staples of one particular make suit you, and your oboe, better than others. The average length of a staple is 47–49 mm., and for the *whole* reed, when finished, say 72–74 mm. The length must be considered in conjunction with the bore, but as a general rule, the longer the staple the flatter the pitch. Test the bore of staples with the mandrel (a tool described later in this chapter, section 5). The farther up the staple the mandrel will go, the wider the bore of the staple, and the flatter it is likely to be. Make sure that your staples are in good condition: the oval opening at the smaller end

[1] Many players, particularly in America, use the word tube rather than staple.

should not be bent, split or flattened, and the cork should not be worn off the metal.

2. *The vital necessity of using a reed to suit yourself*

There are very few oboists who find each other's reeds entirely comfortable, for since each player's embouchure is different, the choice of the reed must also be a very personal matter, and one man's meat is often another's poison. A beginner is incapable of knowing which reeds are suitable, but would be wise to ask for rather soft ones with a medium aperture. As the embouchure control grows more sensitive, the choice of a reed becomes increasingly important. When you are capable of judging, choose a reed because it is comfortable for *yourself*, and avoid the temptation of trying to use reeds like Mr. So-and-So's in the vain hope that they will help you to sound like Mr. So-and-So!

The ideal reed, when blown in properly and ready for use, should feel entirely comfortable—in fact, it should have the *right resistance to your lip and breath pressure*. In addition, it should have a good quality of tone and reliable intonation all over the compass, an easy attack piano or forte, and a full crescendo and diminuendo anywhere on the instrument. This 'perfect' reed is regrettably rare, but imperfect reeds can often be so greatly improved by skilled attention that it really is worth while acquiring a good technique of scraping them (even if not of making them).

Different oboes often require different types of reeds, so if you change your instrument you may find that you need to modify your reeds slightly. Try to avoid a reed which is too open for you; it will tend to make you pinch with your lips, and the sound will be hard to control and often flat on top notes. Avoid also a reed which has too much resistance (i.e. will not vibrate easily enough) for this may encourage you to force breath through it with the throat muscles. A reed which is too close for you, or one which has too little resistance, will often make you overblow in the effort to get more sound from it by forcing, and you may continually shut it up by gripping it, so that no sound comes at all. Some players use the same reed for every purpose and occasion until that reed's life is finished; others change reeds constantly—even during one piece. I think it sensible to compromise between these two methods. Certain reeds will be infinitely more suitable for chamber music or solo playing, others for a heavy orchestral concert: some for a small hall, some for a large one. Different climates demand varying types of reeds. While it is wise therefore to choose a reed for a concert bearing in mind the place and circumstances, I think it is *un*wise to change reeds during a performance in order to get different results. Preferably know your reed so well that you can get the best possible results from it, and overcome its natural limitations by your complete control over it; you can do so much more with a reed you really *know*. Changing reeds very frequently is apt to disturb the embouchure and make its control less sensitive. On the other hand, it is not satisfactory to stick to the same reed until its life ends, for when you *do* have to change (possibly even without warning, through an accident in the middle of a concert) your embouchure may find it hard to adjust to a new reed. A 'perfect' reed—that sadly rare thing—will be right for any occasion and will be capable of anything, but when its life is over, the change to another reed will be even harder! When you have a good reed, start breaking in some new ones while practising, to prepare for the future.

3. *The process of reed-making*

The oboe reed is made from a particular type of bamboo cane (*Arundo donax*) grown in the South of France—from whence the best quality comes—and in other places with similar climates. The cane should be properly matured, and it varies greatly in quality. It is first sold in tubes, about 4–8 inches in length (the distance between the 'joints' of the bamboo), which vary in diameter approximately from $9\frac{1}{2}$ to $11\frac{1}{2}$ mm. Taking into account such factors as staple, gouging, shaping and scraping, the smaller the diameter of the tube, the more open will the finished reed be. The tube is split into parts which are reduced to a uniform width and length, and then gouged (i.e. planed or hollowed out, nearly always by machine) to a certain thickness. This thickness can vary appreciably and must depend on the choice of the reed-maker, who goes by the type of reed to be made and the kind of cane being gouged. These gouged strips are folded and shaped, and here again the variations in the shape may affect the finished reed. Finally the ends of the cane are thinned slightly: the cane is bound on to the staple, and then scraped and cut until ready for playing.

4. *Advantages and disadvantages of making your own reeds*

(*a*) *Advantages.* Since you know better than anyone which reeds feel most comfortable, you should be able to suit yourself more exactly than any reed-maker—once you have acquired the requisite skill. You are spared the anxious wait for a new batch of reeds when you urgently need them. The knowledge that you *can* make some new reeds will give you confidence in touching up your old ones; when you know how the reed is made and scraped, you can alter or renovate it much more efficiently. You can make a reed for a particular occasion. Once you are skilled enough not to waste cane, making your own reeds is much less costly than buying them ready-made or having them made for you.

(*b*) *Disadvantages.* The greatest one is the *time* spent in making reeds. Reed-making technique needs practice, just as anything else, and this does take a lot of time, particularly when you are learning the rudiments of the art. Even when you are really skilled and comparatively speedy, there is the danger of wasting time by continually trying to make the 'perfect' reed. Rather, practise on the useful reeds you've made, and get used to them. Skill in reed-making or reed-scraping may improve your playing, but no reed—however good—can take the place of regular practice. Even a skilled reed-maker cannot make a really good reed without good cane, and this is often hard to obtain—possibly harder for you than for a professional reed-maker importing in bulk.

Nevertheless, it is my own considered opinion that for experienced players the advantages of making reeds far outweigh the disadvantages.

5. *Materials for making reeds*

The quality of the finished reed must depend on *all* the factors concerned; namely the type and diameter size of the cane, and the gouge, shape, and scrape used. Many reed-makers therefore find it more satisfactory to buy their cane in tube, let it mature if necessary, and then process it themselves. Having picked out the size and type of cane they prefer, they may then experiment with the gouge, shape, and scrape, until they can get the best consistent results. For beginners however, it is advisable to start with cane which has been gouged and shaped. When you have a working knowledge of tying on and scraping, you can then shape your own cane and finally gouge it too. Do not use your own reeds if you are in the very early stages of reed-making *and* oboe playing, for you will not know whether your reed or your technique is at fault.

For making reeds with gouged and shaped cane, you must have the following equipment:

Mandrel. A precision made tool for fitting into the staple to measure it and to hold it firmly while binding on the cane.

Knife. For scraping—made of a good quality hard steel (not stainless).

Cutting block. For use when cutting off the tip of the reed. Must be made of a really hard wood, such as ebony, grenadilla, &c.

Tongue, or plaque. For inserting into the reed while scraping. Small flat piece of metal, oval shaped with pointed ends.

Reel of silk, nylon or fine linen thread. For tying on. This must stand a strong pull without snapping: rayon is useless.

Pencil. For marking the position of the cane on the staple.

Millimetre rule. For measuring staples and reeds.

Goldbeater's skin. For wrapping round the blades of cane to stop the reed from leaking, and on occasions for helping to keep the blades in position.

In addition to the above it would be useful to have the following:

Beeswax. For waxing the thread, to prevent its slipping.

Hone. For sharpening knives; very fine carborundum, &c.

Another knife. For rough scraping, so that you can keep the other really sharp for finishing touches. It is also useful to have a third knife, for cutting off tips.

Fine steel files. For scraping. Files of varying grades may be used as well as knives.

Small nail file (emery board). For levelling the sides of the reed if it has been carelessly shaped, or for narrowing it.

Bottle of 'Newskin', nail varnish or similar substance. For painting

over the winding thread to prevent any wear or unravelling, or to stop a leak there.

Wire. A soft wire, about twice as thick as that used for 15 amp.
fuses.

Pliers (very small size with pointed ends). For applying wire.

6. *Types of scrape*

The part of the cane from the tip downwards which has
been scraped and thinned with the knife after tying the cane
on to the staple, is known as the 'scrape' (or sometimes as the
'lay'). There are many different types of scrape to suit different
embouchures and methods of playing, and the scrape must
also vary according to the type, gouge, and shape of the cane
being used. When you first make your own reeds, start by
trying to copy professional ones, and as you get control over
the knife you can experiment with various types of scrape until
you find which suits you and which gives the best results with
the type of cane you are using.

Try a scrape shaped as the letter V, short or long, a short
or long U, or a W, and see what results you get. Imitate the
average bassoon reed scrape with modifications. Hold a
moistened clarinet reed up to the light, and use this as
a model for the shading of the scrape. Experiment with a
very thin tip, leaving a good deal of thickness behind it and
up the spine to compensate. There are endless possibilities.
As you become more skilled and more knowledgeable you will
naturally use different kinds of cane, and will modify the
scrape to suit their varying qualities.

7. *General suggestions for making, scraping, and touching up reeds*

As you should now realize, each different type of cane,
gouge, shape, and scrape will need slightly different treatment,
so these suggestions must only be regarded as hints to guide
you in your experiments. Remember that cane is a natural
substance and not a manufactured one. Even if two pieces of
cane are taken from the same tube and gouged, shaped, and
scraped identically, they will not produce two *identical* reeds!

(*a*) *Choosing the cane*. Many players like mottled cane, or
cane of a particular colour, but colour and markings are not
wholly reliable guides to quality. In any good cane the bark

(i.e. the outside) is always very smooth and glossy: that of poor cane is ridgy and dull-looking. The grain of the cane should look close and even, inside and outside. When the cane has been soaked, fold it and press it sensitively between your finger and thumb. Bad cane (or insufficiently matured cane, which will also give bad results) will bend over easily like rubber whereas good cane would split under the necessary pressure to bend it. Remember that cane, whatever its quality, will bend *more* easily if gouged thinly. You should be able to feel the spring and resistance of good cane when it is wet or dry without proving its quality by splitting it and wasting it. With a little experience you can tell good cane from bad by the feel of it as you are scraping: good cane dusts off evenly and easily under a sharp knife, bad cane comes away in uneven curls. Your thumbnail pressed firmly on the bark should not leave a dent if the cane is good.

The foregoing paragraph is essentially for the beginner's guidance. The more experienced reed-maker will realize that while some cane is really bad, and useless to *anyone*, other cane may seem bad because it is unsuitable for him personally. The really first class hard cane which may be one player's ideal will be useless to another player who likes a soft cane.

(*b*) *Soaking the cane.* This may be varied according to the quality and type of cane used. Soft and rather woolly-sounding cane is sometimes best left overnight in cold water, which may help to harden and brighten it. Personally, I find that soaking in warm (mouth temperature) water for 10–15 minutes is generally satisfactory. The time may be varied slightly; as a general rule, the thicker the cane is gouged the longer soaking it requires.

Here is a useful way of proving that your cane is ready. When it is first put into water it will rise to the surface even after being pushed to the bottom. When it has soaked long enough it will stay under water. The thicker the gouge, the longer the cane will take to sink, but soft cane will sink more quickly than hard cane of the same gouge.

You can also vary the method of wetting the reeds you are using. When water is available I prefer it to saliva. Dip the reed and leave it until it will 'crow', rather than stand it on its tip in water—unless it is particularly dry. (For what it is worth, one well-known player had a theory that regular use of milk for soaking would mellow new reeds more quickly, and another advocated a solution of honey and warm water!)

(c) *Tying on reeds.* Use a thread which will stand a strong pull without breaking, for the tie-on should be so firm that you cannot shift the cane on the staple. Go to an expert and learn to tie on. It is a simple matter, and one practical demonstration is worth pages of description, or even illustrations. Some reed-makers beeswax the thread before winding, to prevent it slipping: a useful alternative is to wet the thread thoroughly just before using it. When you put the cane on the staple, *always* make a pencil mark on either side of the cane to show you exactly where the staple ends. Stop winding exactly at that point so that the cane is correctly supported by the staple.

Remember that cane is always shaped to be tied on the staple a certain distance. When the cane is placed on the staple at the correct point to suit the shape, the sides of the reed should close easily and evenly one turn of the thread before the end of the staple. When you have discovered this point on one piece of cane, measure it, and you can safely presume that the other pieces in the same batch should be tied on the same distance. Here is a rough guide. With the average shape and staple, the amount of cane left showing beyond the thread (i.e. the end of the staple) when the reed is finished, is approximately one inch (26 mm.) A halfpenny is a useful rough measure.

Tying the cane farther or less far on to the staple will slightly influence the pitch and opening, but any appreciable variation in the point of tying on will naturally disturb the balance of the shape and may adversely affect the finished reed.

Particularly if you are using staples of varying lengths and bores (a practice better avoided) it is vital to consider the total length of the finished reed, in conjunction with the placing of the cane on the staple. The average length of the finished reed is 72–74 mm. (When tying on, allow an extra $\frac{1}{2}$ mm. for cutting off the tip.) A longer reed will be flatter, a shorter one sharper, unless the staple or the shape is wider or narrower to compensate. As a general rule for correct pitch, the wider

E

the shape the shorter the reed must be. Remember that a difference in length of even $\frac{1}{2}$ mm. can make an appreciable variation to the pitch of the reed. The wisest plan is to use staples of the same length and bore, and cane of the same shape, and tie on the cane always to the same point. Thus you achieve consistent results in the pitch of the finished reed, which can be slightly adjusted in the scraping stage.

Wrap on the goldbeater's skin firmly, with plenty of moisture. Nail varnish will protect the thread binding and guard against unravelling or leakage, but do not varnish above the thread lest you stop the cane vibrating freely.

(d) *General hints on scraping.* NEVER attempt to work on a reed when

> (1) You are in a hurry, or feeling impatient.
> (2) Your knife is blunt.
> (3) The reed is dry and (if a used one) not damp enough to play.

Always use a very sharp knife for scraping and for cutting off the tip, and learn to sharpen knives yourself, so that you can keep them in first-class order. Never dig with the knife, or press it into the cane, or try to chip away at the cane. A blunt knife will encourage such faults. Never stop the knife on the reed, but always rotate the wrist so that the knife moves in an arc. Try to keep the knife moving when scraping, learn to scrape across the grain of the cane as well as with it. Practise knife control by making a pencil mark on a useless reed and removing it with as few strokes as you can: do this as often as possible, making the marks on all parts of the reed. Then try *avoiding* a pencil mark while you scrape. As with tying on, if you can get an expert to show you how to use a knife properly, you will more easily acquire scraping technique. The knife should be held firmly but not rigidly in the right hand—the blade supported against or under the left thumb, which rests on the reed. The blades of the reed and the plaque[1] are supported by the left forefinger, and the staple is held firmly by the other fingers on the left hand. The

[1] In order to avoid any confusion between the human tongue and the metal one, I shall, throughout this chapter, refer to the latter as the *plaque*, the alternative word used little in England but almost exclusively in America.

reed should be held level while scraping. Some students find it easier to scrape the reed having the staple on the mandrel.

Scrape in a good light. It is often helpful to see the scrape you are achieving by holding the reed up to a strong light, tip downwards.

Always use the plaque when scraping; except, naturally, in the early stages before the blades of the reed are opened. I prefer to rough-scrape the reed and then whisk the plaque through the blades at the tip to open it, and cut it off neatly later on—rather than cut the tip off while it is still quite thick. Certainly this method is kinder to the edge of the knife, and I find it is much less liable to split the reed.

When cutting off the tip of the reed, always cut on a cutting block made of suitable wood, such as ebony or grenadilla, and make sure that the knife is really sharp. You may have difficulty in making an absolutely straight cut. Have the block on a firm, flat and non-slip surface: look both sides of the knife and keep it straight, so that it forms a right angle with the reed. Don't saw at the cane: press the knife steadily and hard down until you are right through the tip of the reed. You may find it helpful to press on the blade of the knife with the forefinger of your left hand, holding the reed firmly with the other fingers and thumb. A good cutting block should have a slightly rounded surface; try starting the pressure with the knife at one corner of the reed, and then rolling the knife firmly to the other corner. (A sort of 'rocking' action.)

Never risk scraping a reed which is really dry; you may easily split it and thus waste it. A reed is easier to scrape evenly and accurately when it is moist enough to 'crow'.

Get used to judging a reed by its 'crow': with a little experience this should tell you nearly as much as playing on the reed. To make a reed 'crow', put it farther in your mouth than you would for playing, and blow loosely. (If you 'play' the reed with a normal embouchure you should get a squeak, which will also help you to judge the resistance of the reed.) As a general guide, a high, tight crow means that the reed has not been scraped enough; a loose, low crow indicates that it has been overscraped. An unscraped or slightly scraped reed will not crow at all.

Always give a reed the chance to settle and then to 'blow

in' before scraping it too much. When you have tied one on, scrape it until you can play on it. The next day you may find that it has stiffened up: scrape it again and play on it for a little while. Do the same thing each day until the reed ceases to alter. A reed tends to alter more if scraped with a blunt knife which presses into the cane and bruises the fibres. Remember that variations in temperature and humidity will alter the 'feel' of any reed, but particularly a new one. It is ready then for use, and should play without retouching until it starts to deteriorate through wear. (Completed reeds left *unused* will often seem different when you play on them again.) Never be tempted to scrape a reed too much without playing on it for a while. Often it only needs to be 'played in' and will be ruined by over-scraping. If you make your reeds, try *never* to put yourself in the position of making one at the last moment. As a general rule it is most unwise to use a new or untried reed for a concert.

Before you finish scraping the reed *make quite sure that it is not leaking*, for even the smallest leak at the sides of the cane, or through the thread binding can affect its playing quality. Stop the end of the staple with your finger and suck the air out through the tip of the reed. When you remove your lips, an airtight reed should make a little popping sound as the blades of the reed open. If you suspect a leak, dip the tip of the reed in water, hold the tip together with your fingers, and then blow from the other end of the staple: water will ooze out from the place where the reed is leaking, if anywhere. If there is a leak, rewrap the gold-beater's skin carefully, and if the binding is at fault, paint the thread with nail varnish and allow it to dry well. Leaking from the sides of the cane, due to faulty shaping or tying on, can often be cured by levelling the sides with an emery board.

When testing a reed on your oboe, do not play on it aimlessly, but try to discover its weaknesses. Try its pitch. Find out the safety of its attack by playing bottom notes pianissimo and fortissimo; then do the same with the top notes. Make a long crescendo and diminuendo in each register (though remember that a new reed should never be quite as responsive as one which has been blown in). Try slurring down various intervals. Play octaves all over the instrument and test their intonation: the G, A, and C are good notes for this. The middle E and middle G will often feel particularly 'tight' if the reed needs more scraping. The lower G will flatten during a diminuendo if there is too little resistance in the middle of the reed behind the tip. Do one thing to a reed and try the effect of that before scraping anywhere else.

Never scrape off too much at a time; you can always take away more cane from the reed, but you cannot put it back!

(*e*) *Suggestions for improving certain weaknesses.*

(i) *Pitch*. If the general pitch is too *flat*, cut a little off the tip or *very* slightly narrow the sides: if the reed is then too stiff, sharp, or dull in sound, scrape off a little to compensate. If the pitch is too *sharp*, lengthen the scrape or thin the existing scrape at the bottom.

(ii) *High notes and low notes*. If the top notes are sharp, lengthen the scrape: if they are flat, reduce the scrape by cutting a little off the tip, or by narrowing the sides. If the top notes are very dull and thick, scrape the tip slightly, on certain types of scrape the very tip of the tip. Narrowing the sides will brighten and harden the sound as well as sharpen the pitch. If the top notes are too bright and inclined to be sharp, try making the V of the scrape more U-shaped. If the low notes are difficult and 'sticky', thin around the bottom of the scrape, particularly at the sides of it, or on some types of scrape thin each side *just* below the tip, on the 'shoulders' of the reed.

(iii) *Opening*. The opening of the reed is very largely determined by the diameter size of the tube of cane from which that reed was made, and by the gouge and shape used. It cannot therefore be altered radically in the scraping stage, though it can be adjusted slightly.

As generalizations, the smaller the diameter of the tube, and the wider the shape, the more open will be the finished reed. Reed-makers can also influence the opening slightly when tying on the gouged and shaped cane, as described earlier in section 7c.

Here are some suggestions for scraping.

If the reed is too *open*, go lightly over the backbone of the scrape, lengthen or thin the V at the bottom of the scrape, or take the bark of the cane off just below it. Another way to close the opening (and/or weaken a reed which has too strong a resistance, and yet which seems to have been scraped enough elsewhere) is to make a thin line of scraping right down the middle of the reed, starting *below* the scrape and going to the binding. Use a file for this purpose. Avoid making too wide a line of scraping, lest you weaken the reed too much.[1]

If the reed is too *close*, cut a little off the tip. Then try scraping from the sides, leaving a backbone down the middle of the reed; or very slightly lengthen the scrape into a real W shape, leaving the *middle* of the W untouched. Rewrapping the goldbeater's skin very tightly will often help to keep the reed slightly more open by supporting the blades.

The opening of a reed can, I find, be satisfactorily adjusted either way by wiring. Many reed-makers scorn this method, because they think that the wire 'chokes' the reed and stops its natural vibration, but many a reed (otherwise impossibly close or open) can be made usable, and often very comfortable, by using a wire. Some fine players habitually play on wired reeds. (A reed *may* need re-scraping slightly after wiring, because of the altered opening and vibration.) You can open or close a reed before playing on it by holding the blades open or shut with the fingers; this will often help matters slightly and temporarily. Be careful not to do it too violently or you may split the reed, and be sure that the cane is well moistened before so treating it.

(iv) *Uncertainty in attack.* Often the cause of this is inferior cane, but any bumps or unevennesses in the scrape may make the reed uncertain in attacking a note piano and liable to stop abruptly during a diminuendo. If you are using the type of scrape which should taper gradually from base to tip, be sure that the scrape really *is* evenly graduated: if you are using the type of scrape which has a thin tip with thickness behind it and down the spine, be particularly careful to see that the tip is very evenly scraped each side, and nicely shaped as an inverted crescent. Sometimes the most minute amount off a very

---

[1] Many reed-makers make extensive use of files for scraping, in conjunction with knives, particularly in the early stages of making a reed. 'Dutch rush', a ridged tubular plant obtainable at woodwind supply stores, is also used for rubbing off very small amounts of cane when the reed is in its later stages of scraping, or for an old reed which needs 'freeing'.

thin tip will make a noticeable difference to a reed of this type. Try the reed, and the blade which is downwards when the sound is thicker will probably be the blade which needs more scraping to balance the reed properly. Even when both sides are apparently scraped equally, a reed will nearly always play better with one particular side upwards. Always try a reed both ways, and put a mark on the goldbeater's skin to show you which is the better side up.[1]

(v) *Whistling.* A reed which whistles, for instance when attacking a top C sharp fortissimo, may be leaking. Otherwise, the tip may be too thin or too long for the balance of the scrape, and may need a little taken off it.

(vi) *Tone.* The type of tone is partly dependent on the quality of the cane, but it may be affected to a greater or lesser degree by the gouge, shape, and—particularly—the scrape. A reed with too much resistance to the player's natural lip and breath pressure will give too thick, tight and unresonant a sound; one with too little resistance will produce a loose, edgy and thin tone. If the reed is too bright or tinny in sound, and/or too free and 'wild' in playing, increase its resistance by cutting a little off the tip. Try also scraping at the sides, particularly from the bottom of the scrape. Soaking with saliva may help to mellow it, and remember that a bright type of reed sometimes improves greatly with constant playing and will often last well when once blown in. If it is too woolly, dull, or thick in sound, lessen its resistance by freeing the tip, thinning lightly all over the scrape, or up the middle, or at the sides just below the tip. Sometimes the cause of a poor sound may be an unsuitable opening, which would cause the player to grip unnaturally if it is too open, or to push with the breath in the effort to get more sound if it is too close. Even a good player can get a comparatively bad quality of tone from a reed which does not suit his embouchure, and this unsuitability and resulting discomfort is far less controllable and more disastrous for the less experienced and less skilled player.

(vii) *Bubbling.* If a reed seems to hold water so that it sounds bubbly, the cane is probably immature. Reed-makers

---

[1] It is salutary and helpful to look at and even to scrape your reeds through a magnifying glass. A watchmaker's eyeglass is useful as your hands are left free while using it.

can help this fault before tying on by sandpapering gently *inside* the cane when it is dry, using a piece of fine sandpaper wrapped round a pencil, and then washing the cane well. Incidentally, this light sandpapering is a very good general practice, likely to improve the finished reed. If only the *bottom notes* sound bubbly, the cause is probably too tight an embouchure—not a faulty reed.

8. *Reviving reeds*

A good way to revive an old or tired reed is to clean it thoroughly.[1] There are several ways of doing this. I find it most effective to put a drop of surgical spirit on a very small feather and twirl the feather gently around inside the reed and up through the tip. (A wing feather of a partridge is ideal for this purpose as it is not too hard or stiff.) Alternatively, put a drop of the spirit into the staple and blow this through the reed. Another method is to leave the reed dipped for five minutes in a solution of peroxide and warm water—about a teaspoonful of peroxide to an eggcupful of water—and then flush the reed by holding the cork end of the staple under a fast-running cold-water tap so that the water runs right through the reed. Some players prefer to use a strong solution of soap and warm water instead of peroxide and water. Another way of removing deposits inside a reed is with a piece of clean, strong paper. A crisp new banknote is ideal! Put a corner of the paper carefully into the tip of the reed and work it down between the blades: then hold the tips of the blades firmly together with the fingers of one hand, while pulling the paper slowly out between them with the other. You can also remove deposits with the plaque, working the dirt out through the sides of the reed. Cleaning a reed in these ways will make it more lively and responsive, at any rate for a little while. An old reed which has been a good one but which is past its best, will often continue to give service if it is used only occasionally—the rest seems to revive it. You can often give an old reed a short new lease of life by cutting a little off the tip, and then re-scraping to compensate for this. Old reeds which

[1] Women oboe players should realize that lipstick clogs the fibres of the cane and may thus spoil a reed. It should be completely removed before playing.

are inclined to be too close may be improved by wiring.

Always keep your reeds in a suitable case, so that you avoid accidental damage to them as much as possible, and never try to play on a dry reed. Wait till you can 'crow' it before using it. Incidentally, you would do well to remember that a reed can dry out very quickly, particularly if the cane is good. Always wet it in your mouth before playing, and suck out any surplus moisture if necessary. Many an untidy orchestral entry is due to the player trying to play on a dry and therefore unresponsive reed. In a very hot or dry atmosphere, some players keep a small jar of water handy, but damping the reed by holding it in your mouth is adequate in normal conditions.

Clean the reed before putting it away after playing. Suck up some fresh water into it and then blow the water through it from the staple end. This will help to prevent the formation of deposits due to saliva and dirt, and so will prolong the life of the reed.

Let me end this chapter with a word of advice. Always get a large part of your daily practice done, if not all of it, *before* starting to work on reeds. If you begin the day with reeds it will be fatally easy not to practise the oboe at all, and as I have already said, the best reed in the world will not take the place of practice. Remember also that it is a bad workman who blames his tools. Admittedly the reed can make life much easier or harder for you, but do not get into the bad habit of blaming it for shortcomings which are really due to your own lack of technique.

VII

PRACTICE

1. *The need for regular practice*

Practising and playing are very different functions. When you play (in public, privately with other people, or even by yourself), you may sacrifice—consciously or unconsciously—certain details for the effect of the whole. For instance, if you are in an orchestra, other instruments playing at the same time as yourself may cover up imperfections in your own technique of which you may not be aware. You may, even when playing quite by yourself, be too carried away by the musical pleasure of what you are doing to listen critically enough to small technical faults, particularly to careless intonation. The purpose of real practice is to acquire complete co-ordination and control of the muscles you need, by conscious and concentrated mental discipline. *No* slip or fault, however slight, must be allowed to pass. Train your ears to observe imperfections, and use your brain to put them right.

2. *How to practise*

(*a*) *The importance of frequent short periods of work.* Practice needs the utmost concentration, and can be very tiring—particularly for those who are unaccustomed to it. Practise as little and as often as you possibly can, so that you may be mentally and physically fresh through each short period. An hour spent in purposeless repetition and in thoughtless mechanical moving of your fingers will do you far less good than twenty minutes of intelligent concentrated work. As you become more used to practising, your powers of concentration and your mental and physical endurance will naturally improve. At first, however short a time you have been at work, do not continue if you find that your attention persistently wanders despite your most intense efforts to prevent this, nor if your embouchure begins to feel so tired that you are unable to control it normally.

(*b*) *The value of slow practice*. The more slowly you practise
a passage, the more quickly and evenly you will ultimately
be able to play it. When you are playing a series of notes
really slowly your ear can easily detect even tiny faults, and
you can concentrate carefully on putting them right. Quicker
playing does not give your brain or muscles time to be so
thorough. Continually playing a passage up to time will have
very little improving effect, and this is really a most wasteful
way of working. If you find it an irresistible temptation to try
the phrase quickly 'just to see how it is getting on', make up
your mind to play it very slowly and critically at least ten
times first!

(*c*) *Practising to overcome weak spots*. When you are aware that
you have a stumbling place or uneven spot in a scale, exercise,
or piece, try to concentrate your practice there, instead of
wasting time by going over and over the whole passage, always
hesitating in the same place. Make little exercises for those few
difficult notes and concentrate on them for a while: *then* try
the whole passage around them. For instance, the scale of D
major over two octaves is quite a simple one, but the part of
it over B, C sharp and D in both octaves is apt to be untidy
and out of tune. Help to overcome this weak spot in the scale
by doing exercises such as this (repeat each bar several times
separately before playing the exercise through):

Invent your own exercises to overcome your particular
difficulties.

(*d*) *Working at stubborn difficulties*. Sometimes a passage will not come right even after much slow and careful practice. The reason may be that your powers of concentration on those few notes have become stale, and therefore less effective. Often if you can leave the passage completely for a while and return to it later, you will find that you can play it quite easily, but unfortunately such a procedure is not always practicable. A change of approach will often help. Try playing the notes slowly, but with different articulations; for instance, practise a legato phrase staccato, and vice versa, or use varying combinations of slurring and tonguing. Practise the notes in different rhythmic patterns; phrase in groups of three notes instead of four or vice versa; play in a dotted rhythm instead of a smooth one or the other way round. Practise a passage a semitone then a whole tone higher, and then lower. The original passage will afterwards seem easier by comparison! A useful way of practising is to play the last note of the difficult passage, then add one note before the last, then two notes, and so on until you have worked back to the first note concerned. These varying ways of practising should be used regularly for troublesome spots. Playing a passage in different ways is an excellent means of finding out how well you really know it. Incidentally, it is my own experience that a difficult passage is never absolutely safe in performance until I can practise it from memory.

(*e*) *General weaknesses.* Try to be aware of your own general technical deficiencies and give more time to them, so that your technique becomes sound all through. The routine of your regular practice must never become stereotyped, but must be varied according to your needs.

(*f*) *The use of a metronome.* Practising *always* with a metronome is inadvisable, because it tends to leave your own vital rhythmic sense undeveloped, and the clicking sound may obscure detail, but the metronome is a most valuable means of checking your way of playing and practising, and it will help to prevent your getting into some bad habits. Use it often when practising to make sure that you are really playing as evenly and as rhythmically as you think. You will be surprised to find that you are consistently hurrying or dragging in unexpected places, or perhaps taking too long over a breath, &c. As I mentioned earlier, the metronome is most useful for quickening your tonguing. A tape recorder can also be most helpful in the final stages of preparing a work, but beware of using it too much while practising lest it become a time waster.

3. *What to practise*

(a) *Scheme of practice*. It is wise to have a general scheme of practice, dividing your time into working at scales, exercises, studies and pieces, &c. This must vary according to the total time available each day, your personal physical and mental capacity for work, and your own weaknesses and particular needs for study. The beginner will be able to practise less than the advanced player because the muscles will get much more easily tired. As a general guide for the average student I would suggest three hours a day, divided as follows:

First hour. Scales, starting with at least ten minutes of slow scales.

Second hour. Exercises and studies, starting with long notes and embouchure exercises such as those given in Chapter II.

Third hour. Pieces, and other work such as orchestral solos, ensemble parts, &c., with the last fifteen minutes sight-reading.

Many students will find that they can comfortably and usefully manage a good deal more in a day, but it would be wise always to divide the time into periods preferably of not more than an hour and much less for a beginner. Take five minutes' break during the practice period if you find your embouchure is getting tired or your mind wandering. You must make your own scheme of practice conscientiously, according to your capacity and your individual opportunities and needs.

(b) *Scales.* They are the backbone of your technique and therefore of your practice. Nothing will improve your playing as much in a short time as regular work at scales. Start the day always with legato slow scales without vibrato: these are invaluable for practising because they will improve your breathing, embouchure control, tone, intonation, and finger movements—all at the same time. Remember that even while playing at the slowest speed, your fingers should still move together cleanly and quickly. Learn your scales if necessary from a book,[1] *but it is essential to memorize them as soon as you can, and always to practise them from memory.* When you have learnt them all thoroughly, you should make a regular plan for your daily scale practice. I would suggest that each day you take one scale and the chromatic scale and practise them in different ways. Work at the scales legato, staccato, in groups of four and of three, forte, piano, with a crescendo up to forte at the top and a diminuendo down to piano at the bottom. Practise them with varying articulations and rhythms, such as the following. (These short examples should be practised up and down the *whole* scale in every key; major, minor, and chromatic.)

[1] E.g., *A Book of Scales for the Oboe*, Rothwell (O.U.P.). This book gives *all* the scales written out in different ways, as well as exercises and practice charts. There is a section for beginners, but the rest is intended for students in the elementary and advanced stages.

Practise the scales in thirds—again in different ways—and work at them in thirds the other way round, i.e.:

as well as the more usual

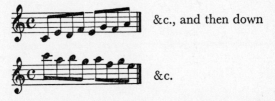

Practise all the scales over two octaves, starting them below their key note where necessary; for instance, play A minor starting on the low C and going up to the top F. Beginners should stay within the compass between the low B flat and the top C; more advanced players should extend their range at least to the top F sharp.

Start on the first day with C major: on the next two days work at A minor harmonic and melodic: then F major, &c.,

through the flat scales (one major, or one of its relative minors, each day). Then go through the sharp scales in the same way and then start again with C major, and so on. In addition, practise the chromatic scale *every* day. As you become more proficient, you can work at more scales on each day and in different ways.[1]

Practise scales frequently with a metronome and increase the speed of all of them equally. Resist the temptation to rattle off C major very quickly while you still stumble slowly over G sharp minor. You can give yourself an incentive if you use a chart—on which you can check off scales as you practise, and make notes of metronome speeds, &c.

(*c*) *Exercises.* In addition to those which you make yourself around difficult spots, which we might call the 'five-finger exercises', you should use regularly a book of simple exercises for embouchure control and articulation, such as one of the following:

Sellner: Part 2 of *Method for Oboe* (Costallat).
Salviani: Vol. 2 of *Method for Oboe* (Ricordi).
Langey: pp. 58–74 of the *Tutor for Oboe* (Boosey & Hawkes), quoted mainly from Sellner.

These exercises are conventional and musically very uncomplicated, so that the notes can be read easily at sight by the more advanced student. This makes it possible to concentrate entirely on *how* the notes are played, and if you practise the exercises carefully as part of your routine, they will effectively improve the control, not only of your embouchure and tongue, but also of your fingers and intonation. Play them slowly at first and increase the speed only when you can do so still playing them flawlessly. When you feel sure of one exercise, practise it also with varying articulations and rhythms. They are an excellent means of limbering up or getting into condition, even for the advanced player. Practise exercises also for specific technical problems—for instance, those given in the earlier chapters of this book for improving embouchure, breathing, and tongue control—and try to

[1] For more advanced students, *La Technique du Hautbois* (in three parts), Bleuzet (Costallat); *Exercices sur les Gammes, les Intervalles et le Staccato*, Gillet (Leduc).

make combinations of these, such as the following, which would be particularly useful for control of the tongue and embouchure:

&c., then down

For practising trills play the two notes slowly and evenly, and use different rhythms, so that you put the musical emphasis on different notes and thus make the fingers even. Thus:

Arpeggios and broken chords are most useful, particularly for embouchure and intonation control. They should be practised daily in conjunction with scales. The following exercise, in all keys, is a useful one.

F

After F major and minor, do it thus:

(d) *Studies.* In addition to scales and exercises, studies should be part of your regular practice system. They will help to improve all branches of your technique, and since they are longer and musically more complicated than the exercises, they will tax your powers of concentration and improve your mental discipline. Work at part of the study at a time and perfect it bit by bit before attempting to play the whole. Do not try to go on and on without taking a breath: set yourself regular and reasonable musical places to stop and breathe out and in properly, and then go back a few notes when you start again so that you never miss an awkward juxtaposition of notes by taking a breath. Always choose (if they are not chosen for you) studies within your technical scope, so that you can really play them well after careful practice. Observe carefully all dynamic markings: it is all too easy to acquire the lazy habit of playing everything at a comfortable mezzo forte. Do not attempt to 'get through' studies which are really too advanced for you. Some of the more difficult ones, for instance Gillet's, are nearly impossible to sight-read, and they remain hard to play accurately even after a lot of practice. They are extremely taxing mentally and physically, and are really suitable only for players with a good groundwork of general technique. Trying to play a study or a piece beyond your capabilities may do you more harm than good. While the majority of studies are written in faster speeds, and are intended primarily for improving the technique of fingers and tongue, slow studies are also most valuable for improving tone and intonation. The studies by Ferling are particularly good in this respect.

For moderately easy studies I would recommend:

Prestini: *Raccolta di Studi* (Ricordi). Particularly the *exercises* in this volume.
Luft: *24 Studies for Oboe* (Costallat).
Brod: *Études et Sonates* (Leduc).
Giamperi: *16 Daily Studies* (Ricordi).

Graduating to:

Lamotte: *18 Studies* (Costallat).
Ferling: *Studies* (Leduc).
Tustin: *Technical Studies for Treble Woodwinds* (Peer International Corp., U.S.A.).
Gillet: *Studies for the Advanced Teaching of the Oboe* (Leduc).

Other useful studies of varying grades have been written by Prestini, Loyon, Salviani, Barret, Karg-Elert, and others. An excellent compendium of technical and orchestral studies is the *Vade-mecum of the Oboist*, by A. J. Andraud (pub. Andraud—Southern Mus. Pub. Co.).

(*e*) *Pieces and Ensemble playing.* Practise the awkward bits of your piece separately as technical exercises, as well as considering it musically as a whole, so that your musical conception is not hampered or trammelled by technical limitations. As I have said earlier, it is advisable to leave your piece until the last period in your scheme of practice, because it will probably be more enjoyable, and therefore easier to practise when perhaps you are getting tired. A well balanced practice schedule is like a well balanced meal with the pieces as 'sweets' or dessert! Think of the piece musically also *away* from the oboe, and try to realize what the composer wants of you. Do not copy *slavishly* any artists however great they may be, and however much you may admire them. Be honest and sincere in your musical thought and interpretation; play a work as you feel it yourself. You should aim to acquire a sense of style so that your playing fits the mood and period of the music. Study music of various kinds (always within the scope of your technical equipment) so that you acquire versatility, musically as well as technically. For instance, learn an eighteenth-century sonata and then work at a contemporary piece, so that your sense of style develops and your musical ideas become flexible. If you find that music of a certain period or style comes more easily to you, work at other kinds, so that you try to overcome a musical limitation. You should practise ensemble playing. Take every opportunity of playing in orchestras of all types and with players of all instruments or with singers, particularly with those who are more advanced than yourself, and train yourself to listen to balance, ensemble, intonation, &c. Practise orchestral passages, so that you may be prepared when you meet them. Books containing important or difficult passages are available—for instance, these:

Bechler-Gumbert, ed.: *Orchester Studien* (Hofmeister).
Heinze, ed.: *Orchester Studien* (Hofmeister).
Bas, ed.: *Etudes d'Orchestre* (Costallat).
Rothwell, ed.: *Orchestral Passages* (Boosey & Hawkes).
Heinze, ed.: *Bach Studien* (Breitkopf & Härtel).
Rothwell, ed.: *Bach Passages* (Boosey & Hawkes).

(*f*) *Sight-reading*. Sight-reading should be practised in rather a different way from scales, exercises, &c. When you are sight-reading, the general impression and the spirit and *rhythm* of the music is more important than the accuracy of details, if you cannot achieve everything—as of course you should with practice. Set yourself a tempo according to the speed at which you think you can play the most difficult passage in the piece, and stick to it. Practise sight-reading with a metronome. Borrow music written for other instruments, for instance for flute or violin, and as you read it, alter the octaves if necessary to make it fit your compass. Try also to practise transpositions, particularly those of a fifth up or down: you may be asked to play a cor anglais part on the oboe, or vice versa.

Duets for two oboes are excellent sight-reading practice. For instance:

Sellner: *Duos* (Costallat).
Luft: *24 Studies in Duet Form* (Carl Fischer).
Telemann: *Sonatas* and *Canons* for two treble instruments. (Schott).
S. Rhys: *6 Inventions* (O.U.P.).

This book was written to help oboe students with their technical difficulties, but I cannot end without a word of warning. If your means of expressing music is the oboe, its problems are naturally of paramount importance to you. But never forget how small a part is played by any one instrument in the vast field of music. Learn to be more critical of your own playing by appreciating the artistry and skill of *all* fine musicians—not only oboe players. Try not to be just an instrumentalist who thinks solely of the oboe, its repertoire, and its reeds. Strive to be a fine artist and a musician who happens to play the oboe.

THE BREATHING MUSCLES

Many laymen talk of the *lungs* as if they were the whole of our breathing apparatus. They are indeed a most vital part of it, but a comparatively passive part. Their work is done *for* them in a sense, by the muscles which alter the size of the chest cavity and thus the pressure within it, thereby causing the lungs to inflate and deflate. The human breathing apparatus may aptly be compared to a pair of fire bellows. The flexible leather bag of the bellows corresponds to the lungs: the metal nozzle communicating to the outside air is the equivalent of our human air passages (nose, throat, &c.). Opening the bellows ('inhalation') causes the bag to swell and fill with air, just as enlarging the chest cavity makes our lungs expand. Closing the bellows ('exhalation') obliges the bag to empty; consequently, reducing the chest cavity compels our lungs to deflate.

Now we must consider the muscular actions which bring about the changes in the size of the chest cavity. Since this very brief and simplified explanation is being written for the student of music, not of medicine, I shall avoid using technical medical terms as much as is consistent with clarity.

The groups of muscles concerned are the abdominal; the intercostal, and other muscles pertaining to the ribs; and the diaphragm, which is the most important of all. The diaphragm is the flexible partition of muscle and tendon which divides the chest cavity from the abdominal cavity. (The word itself is derived from the Greek, meaning barrier.) It is dome-shaped: the central tendon which forms the arch or vault of the dome rises into the chest cavity.

When we breathe in the muscles of the diaphragm contract and pull on its central tendon, flattening the dome and pushing down the abdominal organs. The ribs are moved upwards and outwards. The space in the chest cavity is increased by these actions and the lungs expand to fill this extra space.

When we breathe out the diaphragm relaxes and becomes

dome-shaped again; the abdominal muscles must often be used to hasten and control the exhalation by pushing the arch of the diaphragm up into the chest cavity. The ribs are pulled downwards and inwards. Consequently the space in the chest cavity is decreased and the lungs recoil to their former restricted size.

The diagrams below may help you to understand this explanation.

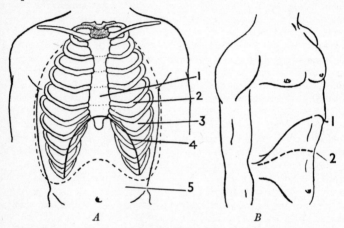

A   *B*

(A) Front position, in which the dotted line shows the lungs expanded to fill the increased capacity of the chest cavity, caused by the movement of the ribs and the flattening of the diaphragm.

1. Breastbone
2. Rib
3. Intercostal muscle
4. Diaphragm
5. Abdominal muscles

(B) Side position.
1. Diaphragm relaxed and dome shaped, as in exhalation.
2. Diaphragm contracted and the dome flattened, as in inhalation.

PLAYING THE COR ANGLAIS

Some players find that the cor anglais seems to suit them particularly well, others prefer the oboe, but all professionals are expected to own both instruments and to be prepared to play either. The general principles involved in playing the cor anglais are the same as in playing the oboe, but it is sensible to bear in mind the fact that the cor anglais is a larger instrument, and in order to play it well, certain slight modifications of control are necessary. You will soon learn to make these sensitive adjustments naturally as you get used to the instrument, but do not expect to become a first-class cor anglais player by practising the oboe.

(a) Control of the air stream

Because it is a bigger instrument than the oboe and has a bigger reed, the cor anglais uses a slightly larger air stream, at a relatively lower pressure. Accordingly the breathing and embouchure muscles must sensitively modify their control. Certain aspects of playing are harder than on the oboe, others are simpler. For instance the control of tone, dynamics, and intonation is easier on the low notes of the cor anglais, but more difficult in the upper register. The natural range of dynamics is smaller than that of the oboe, and the variations of tone colour are more limited.

(b) Reeds

Most players will agree that reeds are less of a problem for the cor anglais player. The reed is larger, and the cane used for it is of a thicker gouge. You will probably find that it needs more 'blowing in' before it is ready for use at a concert, but that it will last longer. As a general rule use a slightly thicker reed and a more open one than you would for the oboe, to accommodate the larger air stream and correspondingly slacker embouchure. Wire is regularly used to control the opening; adjusting this may sometimes alter the quality of sound.

(c) Crooks

A crook can often make a great difference to the tone and/or the intonation of an instrument, as well as to its pitch. If your cor anglais is unsatisfactory, it is worth the experiment of playing it with various crooks before discarding or altering the instrument itself. Wet the top of the crook in your mouth before putting the reed on it, if the reed has a tendency to slip off. If the reed still slips, you may find it necessary to ask an instrument repairer to roughen the end of the crook slightly, but first make sure that the staples you are using are of the correct bore to fit the crook properly. In cold weather always keep the crook warm before playing, in order to prevent excessive condensation of moisture in it from your warm breath.

(d) Pitch and intonation

The cor anglais, being larger, needs more warming than the oboe before it is up to pitch in a cold atmosphere, and unfortunately the oboe player is often expected to pick up the cor anglais and to play a solo on it without being able to warm the instrument beforehand. Remember that the tone of the cor anglais is naturally less bright than that of the oboe, and its sombre quality may tend to make it sound even flatter to the ear than is actually is. It is a good plan therefore to have a *short* crook, which would make the cor anglais play appreciably sharp when warm: you will then be comfortably in tune on the cold instrument, even in conditions when you would be painfully flat with its normal crook. You may *flatten* the pitch by pulling out the crook. As I have said, intonation may be improved by using another crook. The general quality all over a good modern instrument is generally excellent, but an older cor anglais may often have certain poor notes with any crook.[1] The middle C is usually inclined to be flat; too thin or too close a reed will accentuate this tendency. The tone of some notes may not be clear, but woolly or wheezy; the middle C sharp and D sharp, and more rarely the D, are often affected. The quality can sometimes be improved by using the first octave key instead of, or even as well as, sliding or lifting the first finger of the left hand. On

[1] I am referring to the notes as they are *fingered*. They would *sound* a fifth lower in pitch.

some instruments a poor middle E may be improved by using this finger instead of the octave key. The top notes are frequently thin and inclined to be 'wild'. With certain systems of keywork, it is often possible to steady them by putting down one or more right hand fingers. (This also applies to the oboe, but to a lesser degree.) For instance you may flatten and steady the top A by putting down the second finger of the right hand, or the top C by opening the low C natural key. Experiment with your own instrument on these lines: you may discover fingerings to improve the sound of its weak notes.

(e) Choice of instrument and keywork

A cor anglais, particularly an old one, is sometimes made of rosewood, instead of grenadilla or African blackwood which is now normally used. The tone of a rosewood instrument is very sweet and mellow, but smaller; it is less vibrant and does not carry so well. The average cor anglais player often finds it difficult to produce a large, full sound, particularly on the top register. For this reason the blackwood instruments are generally more satisfactory for use in the modern orchestra. The disadvantage of their added weight can be offset by the use of a sling.

It is ideal to have an oboe and a cor anglais of the same wood and make, and with the same system of keywork,[1] but even if you cannot achieve this, try to have as little difference as possible between the two instruments.

Finally, let me repeat that though the cor anglais is so akin to the oboe that it can be played adequately by the average oboe player, it *is* another instrument. You will learn to play it really well only by practising on it. At the same time, bear in mind that practising the cor anglais exclusively may tend to make your oboe tone rather hard, and less controlled. If you must regularly play *both* instruments, divide your practice time between them.

[1] There may be just one discrepancy. It might be wiser not to have the cor anglais equipped with the coupling between the low C sharp or C natural key and the low B natural key (recommended for the oboe in Chapter V, section 1), because, on most instruments, difficulty is experienced in slurring certain notes, particularly D, from the middle to the bottom octave, and this may be overcome by opening the bottom B natural key for the lower note.

A LIST OF MUSIC FOR THE OBOE, OBOE D'AMORE, AND COR ANGLAIS

Since *Oboe Technique* first appeared in 1953 an enormous amount of music for wind instruments has been published, and the music list for this second edition is very much larger than the original one. I have made exhaustive inquiries in the effort to make the present list complete, but it has sometimes proved impossible to obtain accurate information from all the publishers in the many countries concerned. I would not have the temerity to claim that *all* the works available today are included, but I believe that most of them are. I cannot guarantee their musical quality nor the unfailing accuracy of the information concerning them, but I hope that the list is comprehensive and accurate enough to be really useful.

As *Oboe Technique* is widely distributed outside Great Britain, I have endeavoured to trace the actual publisher of every work rather than their agents for this country. Where it has proved impossible to do this with certainty, the name in brackets is that of distributors and may prove a guide in obtaining the work. Where more than one edition is available I have given the publishers concerned in alphabetical order. I have made every effort to omit publications which are out of print and I have not intentionally included any arrangements, other than free transcriptions and piano reductions of orchestral scores.

So many publishers and others have helped me that, regretfully, I cannot take space here to thank them individually, but I do assure them all of my genuine appreciation and gratitude. My particular thanks are due to Hinrichsen, Musica Rara, and United Music Publishers who have patiently dealt with my queries, and to George Rowland, whose own researches into the oboe music repertory have been so generously placed at my disposal.

Readers in Great Britain may find the list of publishers giving nationalities (p. 124), and the following list of agents' addresses, of general guidance in their inquiries. I have not attempted to make it detailed or complete, and I apologize to any firm or agent who may feel that they have been unjustly omitted.

A SHORT SELECTED LIST OF AGENTS IN GREAT BRITAIN FOR MUSIC PUBLISHED ABROAD

BELGIUM: Hinrichsen, 10–12 Baches St., London, N.1.

CZECHOSLOVAKIA: Boosey & Hawkes, 295 Regent St., London, W.1.

DENMARK: J. & W. Chester, 11 Gt. Marlborough St., London, W.1.

FRANCE: United Music Publishers, 1 Montague St., London, W.1.

GERMANY:
{ Hinrichsen, *see above.*
Novello, 160 Wardour St., London, W.1.
Schott, 48 Gt. Marlborough St., London, W.1.

HOLLAND: Lengnick, 14 Sheraton St., London, W.1.

HUNGARY: Boosey & Hawkes, *see above.*

ISRAEL: Chester, *see above.*

ITALY:
{ Hinrichsen, *see above.*
Ricordi, 271 Regent St., London, W.1.

NORWAY:
{ Chester, *see above.*
Hinrichsen, *see above.*

POLAND: Musica Rara, 25 Newport Court, London, W.C.2.

RUSSIA: Musica Rara, *see above.*

SWEDEN:
{ Chester, *see above.*
Hinrichsen, *see above.*

SWITZERLAND: Hinrichsen, *see above.*

U.S.A.:
{ Boosey & Hawkes, *see above.*
Hinrichsen, *see above.*
Mills Music, 20 Denmark St., London, W.1.
Schott, *see above.*

MUSICA RARA specialize in wind music, and in addition to keeping a large stock they will gladly undertake to trace works ordered.

HARRY BAKER, 156 Sutherland Avenue, Welling, Kent, has a comprehensive hire library of music for oboe.

ABBREVIATIONS

r.	Recorder	b.	Bassoon
f.	Flute	contra b.	Double Bassoon
pic.	Piccolo	tp.	Trumpet
o.	Oboe	h.	Horn
o. d'am.	Oboe d'amore	timp.	Timpani
ca.	Cor Anglais	perc.	Percussion
heck.	Heckelphone	tamb.	Tambourine
c.	Clarinet	v.	Violin
bass c.	Bass Clarinet	va.	Viola
alt. sax.	Alto Saxophone	vc.	Cello

vg. Viola da Gamba
db. Double Bass
str. Strings
orch. Orchestra
ch. orch. Chamber orchestra
sop. Soprano
alt. Alto
ten. Tenor
bar. Baritone
p. Piano
ce. Cembalo (Harpsichord)
bc. Basso Continuo
org. Organ
hp. Harp

cel. Celeste
g. Guitar

signs given before works

CA Cor Anglais
O d'am Oboe d'amore
O Orchestral material available
P Piano reduction available

The numbers in brackets after the composers' names refer to the centuries in which they flourished, or flourish.

CONTENTS

I   UNACCOMPANIED OBOE
   Note: Oboe implies the alternative of cor anglais or oboe d'amore in certain works, which are marked *CA* and *O d'am* in *all* sections except *IV*, 1.

II   OBOE AND KEYBOARD INSTRUMENT
   Note: For eighteenth-century works the harpsichord should be used in preference to the piano whenever possible. At that time it was the common custom to reinforce the continuo with a bass instrument—viola da gamba (cello) or bassoon. In many publications a part is provided for this purpose, but as its use is optional I have not specified its inclusion in the lists which follow.
   Works with organ are marked org.

III   OBOE WITH ORCHESTRA (solo or concertante)

IV   CHAMBER MUSIC
   1 Duets and Trios: oboes and cor anglais.
   2 Duets: oboe and various instruments.
   3 Trios without keyboard instrument (see also IV 9).
   4 Trios with keyboard instrument.
   5 Quartets without keyboard instrument (see also IV 9).
   6 Quartets with keyboard instrument.
   7 Quintets for wind (flute, oboe, clarinet, horn, bassoon).
   8 Sextets for wind quintet (as above) and keyboard instrument.
   9 Oboe and strings.
   10 Oboe and voice with one or two other instruments.
   11 A selected list of quintets and larger works for various combinations of instruments.

I. UNACCOMPANIED OBOE

ALESSANDRO, R. d' (20): Op.7a Sonatina (*Sidem*)
ANDRIESSEN, J. (20): Balocco (*Donemus*)
ARBATSKY, Y. (20): Sonata (*Zimmermann*)
BRITTEN, B. (20): Op. 49 6 Metamorphoses after Ovid (*Boosey*)
COLACO, O-S. (20): Sonatina (*Donemus*)
FRANKEN, W. (20): Sonata (*Donemus*)
KRENEK, E. (20): Sonatina für oboe allein (*Bärenreiter*)
MENGELBERG, K. (20): Sonata (*Donemus*)
MÜLLER, G. (20): Sonata für oboe allein (*Sikorski*)
RAINIER, P. (20): Pastoral Triptych (*Schott*)
SCHNEIDER, W. (20): Op. 53 Sonate (*Heinrichshofen*)
SEHLBACH, E. (20): Op. 87 Musik für oboe allein (*Möseler*)
SIGTENHORST-MEYER, B. (20): Landelijke Miniaturen (3 Suites)
(*Alsbach*); Sonatine (*Alsbach*)
WALTERS, L. (20): Syrinx (*Hinrichsen*)
WELLESZ, E. (20): Suite (*Broude*)

II. OBOE AND KEYBOARD INSTRUMENT
O = Orchestral material available

ABSIL, J. (20): Burlesque (*Lemoine*)
ADAMS, W. (20): *CA* Country Scenes (*Schott*)
ADDISON, J. (20): Inventions (*O.U.P.*)
AKIMENKO (19/20): Pastorale (*Bessel*)
ALBINONI, T. (18): Op. 7/3 *O* Concerto in B flat (*Boosey*); Op. 7/6 *O*
Concerto in D (*Boosey*); Sonata in A minor (*Moeck* or *Nagel*)
ALESSANDRO, R. D' (20): works include Op. 67 Sonata (*Foetisch*)
ALEXANDRE, G. (20): Daphnis et Chloe (*Gaudet*)
ALPAERTS, F. (20): Concert Piece (*Metropolis*)
ALWYN, W. (20): *O* Concerto (*Lengnick*)
AMIROW, F. (20): Adagio (*Russian S.P.H.*)
ANDREAE, V. (20): Op. 42 *O* Concertino (*Boosey*)
ANDRIESSEN, H. (20): Ballade (*Donemus*)
ANONYMOUS (17): Suite (*Doblinger*)
ARANYI, G. (20): Romance (*Kultura*)
ARMANDO, G. (20): Op. 11 *O* Concertino (*Schuberth*)
ARNOLD, M. (20): Op. 41 Sonatina (*Lengnick*); *O* Concerto (*Paterson*)
ARRIEU, C. (20): Impromptu (*Leduc*)
ARYTYUNYAN (20): Piece (*Russian S.P.H.*)
AUBAIN, J. E. (20): Air de Ballet (*Leduc*)
AURIC, G. (20): Impromptu (*Noël-Gallet*)
AUSTIN, F. (19/20): Molly Brazen (*Boosey*)
BABELL, W. (18): Sonata in B flat (*Sikorski*); Sonatas in F minor and
G minor (*O.U.P.*)

BACH, C. P. E. (18): *O* Concerto in B flat (*Leuckart*); *O* Concerto in E flat (*Sikorski*); Sonata in G minor (*Ricordi or Breitkopf*)

BACH, J. S. (18): *O* Adagio (Sinfonia, Cantata 156) (*Chester*)

BADINGS, H. (20): Canzona (org.) (*Donemus*)

BALAY, G. (20): Echos d'Armor (*Evette*)

BARAT, J. E. (20): *CA* Nostalgia (*Leduc*)

BARLOW, W. (20): *O* The Winter's Passed (*Eastman*)

BARRAUD, H. (20): Nina au Matin Bleu (*Noël-Gallet*)

BARTHE (19/20): Petite Suite Pittoresque (*Southern*)

BARRE, M. DE LA (17/18): Sonate dite l'Inconnu (*Richli*)

BASSI, L. (18/19): Notturno (*Ricordi*)

BAUER, F.: Suites 1 and 2 (*Moeck*)

BAUMANN, H.: Sonata (*Peters*)

BAYER, J.: Minuet (*Eschig*)

BECHER, H.: *CA* Praeludium (org.) (*Grosch*)

BECK, C. (20): Sonatina (*Schott*)

BELINFANTE (20): Au bord de la Semois (*Delrieu*)

BELLINI (18): *O* Concerto in E minor (*Ricordi*)

BENDA, F. (20): Sonata in F (*Musicus*)

BEN-HAIM, P. (20): Three Songs without Words (*Israeli*)

BENTZON, N. V. (20): Op. 41 Two Pieces (*Hansen*); Op. 71 *CA* Sonata (*Hansen*); Op. 75 *O* Concerto (*Hansen*)

BERGHMANS, J. (20): Pavane (*Noël-Gallet*); *O* Le Labyrinthe (Tableaux Forains) (*Leduc*)

BERNAUD, A. (20): Capriccio Rustique (*Leduc*)

BERTAIN, J. (20): works include Adagio et Scherzo Final (*Lemoine*)

BERTHELOT, R. (20): Air Pastoral (*Leduc*)

BERTHOMIEU (20): Andante et Rigaudon (*Costallat*)

BESOZZI, A. (18): Sonata in C (*Chester*)

BITSCH, M. (20): Romanza (*Leduc*)

BJELINSKI, B. (20): *O* Concerto (*M. Naklada*)

BLÉMANT (20): Sous les Sapins (*Evette*)

BOEHM, Y. (20): *O* Concertino (*Israeli*)

BOISDEFFRE, R. DE (19/20): works include Scenes Villageoises (*Hamelle*); *CA* Elevation (org.) (*Hamelle*)

BOISMORTIER, J. DE (18): Sonata in E minor (*Bärenreiter*)

BONONCINI, G. B. (17/18): Divertimento da Camera (*Moeck*)

BONSEL, A. (20): Suite (*Donemus*)

BORCHARD, A. (20): Pastorale (*Buffet Crampon*)

BORDIER, J. (20): *O* Berceuse (*Durand*)

BORREL, E. (19/20): Habanera (*Durand*); Au Jardin de la flute de France (*Richli*)

BORRIS, S. (20): Op. 48/1 Sonata (*Sirius*)

BORSCHEL, E.: *O* Miniaturen (*Zimmermann*)

G

BOSCOVICH, A. V. (20): *O* Concerto (*Israeli*)

BOTTING: *CA* Pastorale (*Hamelle*)

BOUGHTON, R. (20): *O* Concerto I (*Boosey*)

BOURDENEY, C.: Suite (*Leduc*)

BOURGAULT-DUCOUDRAY: *CA* Les Bergers à la Crêche (*Rouart*)

BOURGIGNON, -F. de: Op. 77 Andante and Scherzo (*Cebedem*)

BOUTRY, R.: Sonatine (*Salabert*)

BOWEN, Y. (20): Op. 85 Sonata (*Chester*)

BOZZA, E. (20): works include *O* Fantaisie Pastorale (*Leduc*); Fantaisie Italienne (*Leduc*); Conte Pastorale (*Leduc*); *CA* Lied (*Leduc*)

BRANCOUR, C. (19/20): *O* Suite (*Buffet Crampon*)

BRETONNIERE, V.: Le Bourdon (Fantaisie) (*Costallat*)

BREVILLE, P. DE (19/20): Sonatine (*Rouart*); *CA* Maneh (*Leduc*)

BROD (19): Several fantaisies and other works (*Choudens* or *Costallat* or *Lemoine*)

BRON, E.: Pastorale (*Costallat*)

BROWN, C. (20): *O* Fantaisie Agreste (*Eschig*)

BRUNS, V. (20): Op. 25 Sonata (*Hofmeister*); Op. 28 *O* Concerto (*Hofmeister*)

BUCHAL, H.: Op. 86 *CA* Sonata (*Breitkopf*)

BUERIS, J. DE: Musette (*Fischer*)

BUSH, A. (20): Op. 42a Northumbrian Impressions (*Novello*)

BUSH, G. (20): *O* Concerto (*Elkin*); Dialogue (*Augener*)

BUSSER, H. (19/20): works include Op. 22 *O* Pièce en Bb (*Leduc*); Op. 84 *O* Asturias (*De Lacour*)

BÜTTNER, M. (20): Improvisationen (*Hofmeister*)

BUXTEHUDE, D. (17): Choralvorspiele (org.) (*Moeck*)

CAINE, E. N. (20): Andante (*Williams*)

CARSE, A. (20): A Dance Measure and Regrets (*Augener*)

CARTER, E. (20): *CA* Pastorale (*Schirmer*)

CASINIÈRE, Y. DE LA (20): Berceuse (*Leduc*)

CASTELNUOVO-TEDESCO, M. (20): Op. 146 *O* Concerto da Camera (*Mills*)

CASTÉRÈDE, J. (20): Intermezzo (Leduc); Sonata (*Leduc*)

CHAGRIN, F. (20): Sarabande (*Lengnick*)

CHALLAN, R. (20): works include Divertissement (*Leduc*)

CHÉDEVILLE, P. (18): Sonatas 3 and 6 (*Richli*)

CHERUBINI, L. (18/19): *CA* Two Sonatas (*Sikorski*)

CHEVREUILLE, R. (20): Op. 75 Pastorale Variée (*Cebedem*)

CILENŠEK: Sonata (*Peters*)

CIMA, P. G. (17): Sonata 2 in D (from Drei Sonaten) (*Sikorski*)

CIMAROSA/BENJAMIN (18): *O* Concerto (*Boosey*)

CLAEZ (20): Andante and Allegro (*Costallat*)

CLÉRISSE, R. (20): works include Fantaisie (*Leduc*)

CODIVILLA, F. (20): Sonata (*Bongiovanni*)

COHEN, S. B. (20): Arioso and Shepherd's Song (*Fischer*)

COLE, H. (20): Slow Air and Dance (*Schott*)

COLIN, C. (19/20): works include 8 Solos de Concours (*Leduc*)

COOKE, A.: Sonata (P or CE) (*Novello*)

COOLIDGE, E. S. (19/20): Sonata (*Fischer*)

CORELLI/BARBIROLLI (17/18): *O* Concerto (*Boosey*)

CORETTE, M. (18): Suite in C (*Ricordi*)

COWELL, H. (20): 3 Ostinati with Chorales (*Presser*)

CURZON, F. (20): A Period Piece (*Boosey*)

DALLIER, H. (19/20): Fantaisie Caprice (*Leduc*)

DAMASE, J. M. (20): *O* Rhapsody (*Lemoine*); Pavane Variée (*Lemoine*);
    Rigaudon (*Lemoine*)

DANICAN/PHILIDOR, A. (17/18): Sonata in D minor (*Barenreiter*)

DANNING, C. (19/20): Solitude (*Hansen*)

DAUTREMER, M. (20): Air Lontain (*Leduc*)

DELCROIX, L. (19/20): Op. 20 *CA* Lied Elegiaque (*Evette*)

DE ROYE, E.: Canzonetta (*Metropolis*)

DESLANDRES, A. (20): Introduction et Polonaise (*Leduc*)

DESPORTES, Y. (20): works include Sérenade des Oiseaux (*Leduc*)

DIÉMER, L. (19/20): Op. 35 Deux Pièces (*Durand*); Op. 52 Légende
    (*Leduc*)

D'INDY, V. (19/20): Op. 31 *O* Fantasy (*Durand*)

DITTERSDORF, D. von (18): *O* Concerto in G (*Breitkopf*)

DOBRODINSKI, B. (20): Concertino (*Sadlo*)

DONATO, V. DE (20): *CA* Pastorale (*De Santis*)

DONJON: Offertoire (*Delrieu*)

DORNEL, L. A. (17/18): Première Suite (*Richli*)

DOUEL: Pastorale Dorienne (*Delrieu*)

DRAEGER, W. (20): 3 Miniaturen (*Hofmeister*)

DRANISCHNIKOW, M.: Poème (*Russian S.P.H.*)

DREJSL, R.: Suite (*Artia*)

DRING, M.: (20): Italian Dance (*Arcadia*)

DUBOIS, P. M. (20): Ballade Médiévale (*Leduc*)

DUNHILL, T. (19/20): 3 Short Pieces (*Boosey*); Suite: Friendship's
    Garland (*Boosey*)

DURAND, A. (19/20): works include Chaconne (*Durand*)

DUTILLEUX, H. (20): Sonate (*Delacour*)

EDMUNDS, C. (20): Andante (*Schott*); Longing for Summer (*Schott*);
    High Summer (*Schott*)

EICHNER, E. (18): *O* Concerto in C (*O.U.P.*); *O* Concerto in B flat
    (*Hofmeister*)

ELLIOTT, M. (20): Three Pieces (*Chester*)

ÉTESSE, E.: Sérenade (*Gaudet*)

ETLER, A.: Introduction and Allegro (*A.M.P.*)

EVANS, P. (20): Sonata (*Chester*)

EYMIEU: Pastorale (*Delrieu*)

FARGUES, C.: Trois Pièces Mignonnes (*Delrieu*)

FAUCHEY, P.: Ballade Hongroise (*Lemoine*)

FAYE-JOZIN, F.: Souvenirs des Moissons (*Lemoine*)

FESCH, W. DE (18): 6 Sonatas (*Bärenreiter*)

FILIPPUCCI, E.: O Elegie (*Enoch*)

FISCHER, J. C. (18): O Concerto in C (*Augener*); Suite in G (*Schott*); Vier Suiten (*Bärenreiter*); Divertissement (*Schott*); Concerto in E flat (*Novello*)

FLÉGIER: Villanelle (*Southern*)

FLEMING, C. LE (20): Air and Dance (*Chester*)

FLOTHIUS, M. (20): Op. 47 Kleine Suite (Vocalises) (*Donemus*)

FORÊT, F.: works include Grave et Allegro Giocoso (*Costallat*); Sonata in G (*Costallat*)

FOSS, L. (20): O Concerto (*Southern*)

FRAIPONT, G.: Marivaudage (*Costallat*)

FRASER, S. (20): Prelude and Scherzino (*Boosey*)

FRENSEL-WEGENER, E. (20): Hobo Suite (*Donemus*); Menuetto (*Donemus*)

FRICKER, P. R. (20): Op. 13 CA O Concertante (*Schott*)

GAÁL, J. (20): Sonata (*Kultura*)

GABAYE, P. (20): Sonatine (*Leduc*)

GAGNEBIN, H. (20): Danse Montagnarde (*Henn*)

GALLIARD (18): Op. 1/1, 2, 3 Sonatas in C, D minor, E minor (*Ricordi*)

GALLOIS MONTBRUN, R. (20): Prélude (*Leduc*)

GANNE, L.: works include Villanelle (*Enoch*)

GARIMOND, H. (19/20): works include Fantaisie Pastorale (*Costallat*)

GAUBERT, P. (19/20): Intermède Champêtre (*Leduc*)

GAULTIER DE MARSEILLE, P.: Suite in G minor (*Richli*)

GEISER, W. (20): Op. 38 Sonatina (*Bärenreiter*)

GEIST, C.: O Andante Pastorale (*Schmidt*)

GEMINIANI, F. (17/18): O Sonata 1 (*Ricordi*)

GENZMER, H. (20): O Chamber Concerto (*Schott*)

GERAEDTS, J. (20): Jan Klaassen Serenade (*Donemus*)

GERMAN, E. (19/20): Pastorale and Bourrée (*Boosey*)

GIBILARO, A. (20): O Fantasy on favourite Airs (*O.U.P.*); Four Sicilian Miniatures (*F.D. & H.*)

GIRNATIS, W. (20): Sonata (*Sikorski*)

GLUCK/BENJAMIN (18): O Divertimento on themes of Gluck (*Boosey*)

GODARD, B. (19): works include Marche Highlanders (*Hamelle*)

GODRON, H. (20): Suite Bucolique (*Donemus*)

GOENS: Scherzo (*Hamelle*)

GOEPFART, K. (19/20): Op. 22 Andante Religioso (*Zimmermann*)

GOLESTAN, S.: *O* Elegie and Danse Rustique (*Durand*)

GOOSSENS, E. (20): *O* Concerto (*Leduc*)

GOVER, G. (20): April Song (*Chester*)

GOW, D. (20): Op. 40 Romance (*Augener*)

GRAM, P. (20): Op. 29 Pastorale and Capriccio (*Hansen*)

GRAUN, J. C. (18): *O* Concerto in C minor (*Sikorski*)

GRETCHANINOFF, A. (20): Op. 138 Brimborions (*Augener*)

GRISELL, R. (20): Pastorale (*O.U.P.*)

GROVLEZ, G. (19/20): Sarabande et Allegro (*Leduc*)

GUILHAUD, G.: works include 1st Concertino (*Costallat*)

GUILLOU, R.: *CA* Sonatine (*Leduc*)

HAAS, J. (20): Op. 23 A Garland of Bagatelles (*Schott*)

HAEYER, F. C. D': Pastorale (*Metropolis*)

HAMERTON, A. (20): Three Pieces (*Augener*)

HANDEL, G. F.: (18): Two Sonatas: G minor and C minor (*Leduc* or
    Peters or *Ricordi* or *Schott*); Sonata in B flat (*Schott*); *O* Concerto
    8 in B flat; *O* Concerto 9 in B flat; *O* Concerto 10 in G minor
    (*Boosey* or *Breitkopf* or *Leduc* and others)

HANSCHKE, H. G.: Sonatine (*Schott*)

HANSON, H. (20): Op. 38 Pastorale (*Fischer*)

HARTY, H. (20): Chansonette (*S. & B.*); À la Compagne (*S. & B.*);
    L'Orientale (*S. & B.*)

HAUG, H. (20): Prélude et Rondo (*Leduc*); Élegie Pastorale (*Henn*)

HAYDN, J. (18) (attrib. to): Concerto in C (*Breitkopf or O.U.P.*)

HEAD, M. (20): Three Pieces (*Boosey*)

HERVELOIS, D'. (17/18): Suite (*Delrieu*)

HESSENBERG, K. (20): Op. 71/2 Capriccio (*Leduc*)

HIDAS, F. (20): *O* Concerto in D (*Kultura*)

HILLEMACHER, P. (19/20): Villanelle Archaique (*Lemoine*)

HINDEMITH, P. (20): Sonata (*Schott*); *CA* Sonata (*Schott*)

HLOBIL, E. (20): Op. 26b Andante Amabile (*Artia*); Allegro leggiero
    (*Artia*)

HÖFFER, P. (20): Op. 43 Serenade (*Litolff*); Op. 45 *CA* Concerto
    (*Kistner and Siegel*)

HOFMANN, R. (19/20): 10 Melodische Vortragsstucke (*Hofmeister*)

HOLBROOKE, J. (19/20): *CA* Ballade (*Modern Music Lib.*)

HOLFORD, F. (20): works include Dance for a Gnome (*Chester*)

HOLLINGSWORTH, S. (20): Op. 2 Sonata (*Schirmer*)

HOLÝ, J. (20): Serenade (*Otto*)

HOROVITZ, J. (20): Op. 3 Sonatina (*Mills*)

HOTTETERRE, J. (17/18): Suite in D (*Ricordi*); Op. 71/2 Sonata in D
    (*Richli*)

HOUDY, P.: Prelude (*Leduc*)

HÜE, G. (19/20): Petite Pièce (*Leduc*)

HUGHES-JONES, L. (20): Elegy and Scherzo (*Chester*)

IBERT, J. (20): *O* Escales 2 (*Leduc*); *O* Symphonie Concertante (*Leduc*)

INDY, V. D'. (19/20): *see under* D'INDY

JACOB, G. (20): *O* Concerto 1 (*Williams*); *O* Concerto 2 (*Williams*); *CA O* Rhapsody (*Williams*); Sonatina (P or CE) (*O.U.P.*)

JELESCU, P.: Sonatina (*Rumanian S.P.H.*)

JOLIVET, A. (20): Chant pour les Piroguiers de l'Orenique (*Noël-Gallet*); Sérenade (*Costallat*)

JONGEN, L. (20): Humoresque (*Leduc*)

KABELÁČ, N.: Sonatina (*Artia*)

KALABIS (20): Op. 26b Suite (The Bagpiper) (*Artia*)

KENNAWAY, L.: *O* Interrupted Serenade (*Hinrichsen*)

KIRNBERGER, J. B. (18): Sonata in B flat (*Sikorski*)

KISIELEWSKI, S. (20): Suite (*Moeck*)

KOECHLIN, C.: *CA* Piece (*Salabert*); Sonata (*McGinnis*)

KOETSIER, J. (20): Op. 41/1 *CA* Partita (org.) (*Donemus*)

KONINCK, S. DE (KONING) (18): Sonatas 7, 9, 10 (*Moeck*)

KONRAD, G.: Easy Pieces (*Hofmeister*)

KORCHMAREV, K. A. (20): *CA* Turkmenian Melody (*Russian S.P.H.*)

KORN, P. J. (20): Op. 7 Sonata (*Simrock*); Op. 14 *O* Rhapsody (*Simrock*)

KREBS, J. L. (18): 8 Choral Preludes (org.) (*Presser*); Fantaisie in F minor (org.) (*Breitkopf*); Kammersonaten 14 (*Breitkopf*)

KRONKE, E. (19/20): Op. 160 Suite im Alten Stil (*Zimmermann*)

KROMMER (KRAMÁŘ), F. (18/19): Op. 37 Concerto in F (no orchestral material available) (*Artia*); Op. 52 *O* Concerto in F (*Artia*)

KUBIZEK, A. (20): Sonata (*Doblinger*)

KUMMER, F. A. (19): Op. 9 *CA* Two Pieces (*Hofmeister*)

LABATE, B. (20): Habanera and several short pieces (*Fischer*)

LALLIET: works include *CA* Fantaisie originale (*Costallat*); 1st Concert solo (*Costallat*)

LACOMBE, P.: Aubade de la Mariée (*Enoch*)

LAMOTTE, A.: Elegie (*Costallat*)

LAMY, F.: Pastorales Variées (*Durand*); *O* Rustique (*Leduc*)

LAPIS, S. (18): Op. 1/3, 4, 8 Drei Leichte Sonaten in D, A, E minor (*Schott*)

LARA, A.: Granada (*Southern*)

LARSSON, L. E. (20): Op. 45/2 Concertino (*Gehrmans*)

LAURISCHKUS, M. (19/20): Op. 31 Sonate in E minor (*Hofmeister*)

LE BOUCHER, M.: *O* Fantaisie Concertante (*De Lacour*)

LECLAIR, J. M. (18): Op. 7/3 *O* Concerto in C (*Leukhart*)

LEFEBVRE, C. (19/20): Deux Pièces (*Durand*)

LEFTUS, O. (20): *CA* Elegie (*Kudelik*)

LENOM, C.: Canzonetta, Caprice mazurka, Musette (*Gaudet*); Musette (*Southern*)

LEPITRE: Les concours d'Annick (*Lemoine*)

LESCHETIZKY (19/20): Variations on a theme of Beethoven (*Schott*)

LEWANDOWSKA, L. (19): Sonatina (*Ars Polona*)

LOEILLET, J. B. (17/18): Sonata in C (*Chester*); Sonatas in E and G (*Lemoine*); Op. 5/1 Sonata in E (*Mus. Rara*); Book 1, Sonatas in A minor, D minor, G major (*Bärenreiter*); Book 2, Sonatas in B flat, G, C (*Bärenreiter*); Book 3, Sonatas in E minor, C minor, A minor (*Bärenreiter*); Sonatas in F, C, A minor, D minor, E minor (*Moeck*)

LOVREGLIO: L'Appel du Matin (*Delrieu*)

LUIGINI: Romance (*Delrieu*)

MAASZ, G. (20): *O* Concertino (*Sikorski*)

MADLO, V. (20): Op. 1 Romance (*Kotba*)

MACMAHON, D. (20): *O* Concerto (*Goodwin & Tabb*); *O* Northumbrian Suite (*Elkin*)

MADOW, N.: Op. 67/1 Sonatina (*Russian S.P.H.*)

MAGANINI, Q. E. (20): Clair de lune and Valse de ballet (*Fischer*); *CA* Villanelle of Autumn (*Fischer*)

MALIPIERO (20): Impromptu Pastoral (*Leduc*); *CA* Canto nell'Infinito (*Leduc*); *O* Sonata (*Suvini*)

MARCELIN, E.: Andante et Musette (*Leduc*)

MARCELLO, B. (18): *O* Concerto in C minor (*De Wolfe* or *Forberg* or *Zanibon*); 4 Sonatas in F, D, D minor, G minor (*De Santis*)

MARECZEK, F.: *CA* Sommerabend am Berg (Impression) (*Zimmermann*)

MARTELLI, H. (20): Op. 71 Adagio, Cadenza and Final (*Eschig*)

MARTINU, B. (20): *O* Concerto (*Eschig*)

MASON, J.: Tenuto (*Elkan*)

MATĚJ, J.: *O* Sonata de Camera (*Artia*)

MATTHES, K. L.: Sonata in C (*Sikorski*)

MATZ, A. (20): Sonata (*Peters*)

MAUGUE (20): Pastorale (*Costallat*)

MENGELBERG, K.: Sonata (*Donemus*)

MERSSON: Caprice (*Henn*)

MESQUITA, C. DE.: Chanson de la Esmeralda (*Lemoine*)

MEUNIER, G.: Andantino (*Philippo-Gallet*)

MEZZACAPO, E.: works include Tristesse (*Gaudet*)

MIELENZ, H.: Schelmische Amoretten (*Ries & Erler*)

MIGOT, G. (20): Sonate à Danser (La Malouve) (*Leduc*)

MIHALOVICI (20): Op. 13 Sonatine (*Eschig*)

MILHAUD, D. (20): *O* Sonatine (*Durand*); Concerto (*Heugel*)
MILLET, A.: A vol de l'oiseau (*Hofmeister*)
MILWID/KRENZ (18/18): *O* Sinfonia Concertante (*Moeck*)
MOLIQUE, B. (19): *O* Concertino in G (*Breitkopf*)
MONFEUILLARD, R.: Mélopée et Scherzo (*Costallat*)
MOORE, T.: *CA* Andante (*Schott*)
MOREAU: Évocations Rythmiques (*Costallat*); *O* Pastorale (*Evette*)
MORRA: Romantique (*Fischer*)
MORTENSEN, O. (20): Sonata (*Hansen*)
MOUQUET, J.: Op. 31 Bucolique (*Evette*)
MOZART, W. A. (18): K. 314 *O* Concerto in C (*Boosey*)
MULDER, H. (20): Op. 79 *CA* Sonata (*Donemus*); Op. 39 and 43 Sonatas 1 and 4 (*Donemus*)
MÜLLER, B. E.: Op. 12 *CA* Abendempfindung (*Grosch*)
MÜLLER, S. W. (20): Op. 52 Sonata in E flat (*Breitkopf*)
MÜLLER-LAMPERTZ, R.: Kleines Konzert (*Grosch*)
MURGIER, J. (20): *O* Concerto (*Lemoine*); Capriccio (*Noël-Gallet*)
NAUDOT, J. J. (18): Première Fête Rustique (*Richli*)
NAUMANN, E. (20): Variationen Suite (*Peters*)
NAVÉ, A. R.: works include The Cuckoo (*Fischer*)
NEMIROFF, I. (20): *O* Concerto (*McGinnis*)
NICHOLAS, M. (20): Melody (*Chester*); Rhapsody (*Chester*)
NIELSEN, C. (19/20): Op. 2 Zwei Fantasiestücke (*Hansen*)
NIVERD, L.: 6 Pièces Brèves (*Philippo-Gallet*); Pastourelle (*Delrieu*)
NOVAK, J. (19/20) *O* Concerto (*Artia*)
NOYON, J. (20): Concertino Pastorale (org.) (*Procuré du Clergé*)
PAINTER, P. (20): *O* Petite Pastorale (*Fischer*)
PALADILHE, E. (19/20): Solo (*Heugel*)
PARROTT, I. (20): Minuet (*Schott*)
PARTZKHALADZE, M.: Two pieces (*Russian S.P.H.*)
PASCAL, C.: Pièce (*Durand*)
PASFIELD, W. R.: Two Pieces (*Williams*)
PASSANI: Pastorale (*Philippo-Gallet*)
PAUER, J. (20): Capriccia (*Artia*); *O* Concerto (*Artia*)
PEDROLLO, A. (20): *O* Concertino (*Zanibon*)
PELLEGRIN, N.: works include Melodie (*Costallat*)
PEPUSCH, J. C. (17/18): Sonatas 1-8 (*Moeck*)
PERGOLESI/BARBIROLLI (18/20): *O* Concerto on themes of Pergolesi (*O.U.P.*)
PÉRILHOU, A.: Passepied (*Heugel*)
PETIT, A-S.: Doux Rêve and other short pieces (*Gaudet*)
PETRIČ, I.: Sonatina (*M. Naklada*)
PFEUFFER, W.: Minuet (*Grosch*)
PIERNÉ, G. (19/20): Op. 5 Pièce en sol mineur (*Leduc*)

PISK, P. (20): Works include Op. 86/2 Idyll (*A.M.P.*); *O* Shanty Boy (*A.M.P.*); Suite (*Southern*)

PISTON, W. (20): Suite (*Schirmer*)

PITFIELD, T. (20): Sonata (*Augener*); Rondo Lirico (*O.U.P.*)

PLANEL, R. (20): Comme une Sérenade (*Noël-Gallet*); Prélude et Danse (*Leduc*); Chanson Romantique (*Leduc*)

PLATONOV, G.: Sonata (*Russian S.P.H.*)

PLATTI, G. B. (18): Sonata in D (*Russian S.P.H.*)

POOT, M. (20): *O* Capriccio (*Cebedem*)

PORRET, J.: Concertinos 13 and 14 (*Costallat*)

POSER, H.: Op. 9 Sonata (*Sikorski*)

POVIA, F.: Three Easy Pieces (*M. Naklada*)

PRESTINI, G. (19/20): Concerto (*Bongiovanni*)

QUANTZ, J. J. (18): Sonata in D (*Bärenreiter*)

RAASTED, O. (20): Sonatina (*Skandinavisk*)

RAKOV, N.: Sonata (*Russian S.P.H.*)

RALSTON, A. (20): Three English Folk Tunes (*New Wind*)

RAPHAEL, G. (20): Op. 32 Sonata (*Breitkopf*); Op. 65/2 Sonata (hp. or p.) (*Breitkopf*)

RASSÉ, F. (19/20): *CA* Cantabile (*Rolland*)

RATEZ, E. (19/20): Op. 13 Cinq Pièces (*Lemoine*)

RAWSTHORNE, A. (20): *O* Concerto (*O.U.P.*)

REIZENSTEIN, F. (20): Op. 11 Three Concert Pieces (*Boosey*); Sonatina (*Lengnick*)

REUSCHEL, A.: Ballade (*Lemoine*)

REUTTER: Pastorale de Noël (*Leduc*)

RICHARDSON, A. (20): works include French Suite (*O.U.P.*); Op. 22 *CA* Three Pieces (*Augener*)

RÍDKY, J.: Op. 26a Ukolébavka (*Sadlo*)

RIEGGER, W. (20): Op. 35 Duos (*Presser*)

REITHMÜLLER, H.: Op. 41 Kleine Hausmusik (*Mitteldeutscher*)

RIETZ, J. (19): Op. 33 Konzertstück (*Breitkopf*)

RISINGER, K.: Sonatina (*Artia*)

RIVIER, J. (20): Improvisation et Final (*Leduc*)

ROBBINS, G. (20): Régates (*Leduc*); Sonatina (*Leduc*)

ROESGEN-CHAMPION, M. (20): Nocturnes 1 and 2 (org. or p.) (*Leduc*)

ROMAN, J. H. (18): *O* Concerto in B flat (*Skanton*)

ROPARTZ, J. G.: works include *CA* Adagio (*Rouart*); Pastorale et Danse (*Enoch*)

ROREM, N.: Mountain Song (*Southern*)

ROTA, N. (20): Elegia (*Leduc*)

ROUGNON: Allegro symphonique (*Hamelle*)

ROWLEY, A. (20): Pavane and Dance (*Boosey*)

ROYE: Canzonetta (*Metropolis*)

ROZKOŠNÍ, J. R. (20): works include Nocturne (*Urbenek*)

RUBBRA, E. (20): Op. 100 Sonata in C (*Lengnick*)

RUST, W.: Sonata (or hp.) (*Pro Musica*)

RUYNEMAN, D. (20): Sonatine (*Donemus*); Sonatine CE: (*Donemus*)

RYCHLIK, J. (20): *CA* Study (*Artia*)

SABON, E.: Various fantaisies, &c. (*Lemoine*)

SACHSE: *CA* Sonata (*Peters*)

SAINT-SAËNS, C. (19/20): Op. 166 Sonata (*Durand*)

SAMAZEUILH, G. (19/20): Esquisse d'Espagne (*Durand*)

SAMMARTINI, G. (18): Sonata in G (*Chester*)

SANCAN, F.: Sonatine (*Durand*)

SANDBY, H.: 2 Pieces (*Skandinavisk*)

SANDRÉ, G. (19/20): Pastorale (*Hamelle*)

SANTO LAPIS: Op. 1 Sonata du Camera (*Schott*)

SCARLATTI/BRYAN (18/20): *O* Concerto 1 (*Chester*)

SCHAEFERS, A. (20): Op. 20 *O* Concerto (*Schott*)

SCHILLING, H. L.: Suite (*Moeck*)

SCHINDLER, H.: Op. 38 Sonata (org.) (*Hofmeister*)

SCHLEMM, G. A. (20): Pastorale and Scherzo (*Zimmermann*); Sonatine (*Ries & Erler*)

SCHMID, H. K. (19/20): Op. 34/1 Pastorale (*Schott*)

SCHMITT, F. (19/20): Op. 30/1 Andantino (*Leduc*); *CA* Chant du Soir (*Rouart*)

SCHOLLUM, R. (20): Op. 55/2 Sonatine (*Döblinger*)

SCHOUWMAN, H. (20): works include Sonatines 1 and 2 (*Belwin*)

SCHRECK, G. (19/20): Sonata (*Kahnt*)

SCHROEDER, H.: Op. 34 *O* Concerto (*Müller*)

SCHULLER, G.: Sonata (*McGinnis*)

SCHUMANN, R.: (19): Op. 94 3 Romances (*Augener* or *Breitkopf* or *Peters*)

SCHWENKE, C. (18/19): *O* Concerto in C (*Hofmeister*); Liechte Stücke (*Hofmeister*)

SCOTT, C. (19/20): Concerto (*Elkin*)

SEARLE, H. (20): *CA* Gondoliera (*Schott*)

SEIBER, M. (20): Improvization (*Schott*)

SEMLER-COLLERY, J.: Récit et Scherzando (*Leduc*)

SHINOHARA, M.: Obsession (*Leduc*)

SHISHKOV, G.: 2 Pieces (*Russian S.P.H.*)

SINIGAGLIA, L. (19/20): Op. 19 12 Variations on a theme by Schubert (*Breitkopf*)

SKALKOTTAS, N. (20): Concertino (*McGinnis*)

SOMERS-COCKS, J. (20): 3 Sketches (*Augener*); Sonatina (*Augener*)

SOUDÈRE, H.: Stance et Mouvement Perpetuel (*Eschig*)

SOULAGE, M. (20): Pastorale (*Evette*)

STAHULJAK, M.: Sonatina (on national songs of Herzegovina) (*M. Naklada*); Sonatina (on national songs of Bosnia) (*M. Naklada*)

STAMITZ, C. (18): Concerto in C minor (*Sikorski*)

STANLEY-SMITH, D. (20): Sonata (*S.P.A.M.*)

STANTON, W. K. (20): 2 Pieces (*S. & B.*)

STEIN, E. D.: O Concerto (*Schmidt*)

STEKKE, L.: *CA* Fantaisie Élegiaque (*Gervan*)

STILL, W. GRANT (20): Incantation and Dance (*Fischer*)

STÖLZEL, G. H. (18): O Concerto in D (*Sikorski*)

STRATTON, G. (20): Pastorale Concerto (*Novello*)

STRAUSS, R. (19/20): O Concerto (*Boosey*)

STRIMER, J.: Pastorale Caucasienne (*Durand*)

SUCHÝ, F.: Op. 4 Sonatina (*Artia*)

SWINSTEAD, F. (20): Pastorale (*Williams*)

SZALOWSKI, A. (20): Sonatina (*Amphion*)

TANSMAN, A. (20): Sonatine —

TELEMANN, G. P. (17/18): O Concerto in C minor (*Schott*); O Concerto in D minor (*Sikorski*); O Concerto in E minor (*Sikorski*); O Concerto in F minor (*Peters*); Wedding Divertissement (*Schott*); 15 Stücke (aus 7 mal) und 1 Mennett (*Lienau*); Sonaten und Spielstücke (*Bärenreiter*); Sonata in B flat (*Sikorski*); Sonata in E minor (*Sikorski*); Kleine Kammermusik (*Forberg* or *Bärenreiter*); Sonata in E flat (*Sikorski*); Sonatas in A minor and G minor (*Leduc*); Sonatas in G minor and C minor (*Breitkopf*); Sonata in G minor (*Schott*); 12 Marches—Ein Fröhlicher Tugendspiegel (*Lienau*); 6 Partitas (*Bärenreiter*)

THÉRON, J.: Piece Élegiaque (*Lemoine*)

THILMAN, J. P. (20): Kleine Sonata (*Peters*); Op. 34 *CA* Sonata (*Sikorski*)

TOMASI, H. (20): O Concerto (*Leduc*); Le Tombeaux de Mireille (p. or tamb.) (*Leduc*); O Danse Agreste (*Leduc*)

TOUMA, H.: Samai (*Israeli*)

TRIÉBERT: Air Varié (*Lemoine*)

TROUBAT, G.: Air Gai (*Philippo-Gallet*)

TROWBRIDGE, L. (20): Homage to Chopin (*Elkan*)

TRUDIČ, B.: Sonatina (*M. Naklada*)

URAY, E. L.: Minnelied Variationen (*Doblinger*)

VALENTINE, R. (17/18): Sonatas 1 in F and 8 in G (*Schott*); Drei Sonaten (*Lienau*)

VANHALL, J. (18/19): Sonata (*McGinnis*)

VANHALL/TAUSKY: O Concerto (*O.U.P.*)

VELDE, VAN DE: Romance (*Gaudet*)

VERHAAR, A. (20): Op. 29 Klein Concert (*Donemus*)

VERNON, ASHLEY (20): O Rhapsodie (*Elkan Vogel*)

VERROUST, ST. (19): Various Fantaisies, &c. (*Lemoine*)

VINCENT (18): Sonata in D (*Schott*)

VIVALDI, A. (17/18): works include Sonata in G minor (*McGinnis*); Sonata in C minor (*Schott*); Il Pastor Fido: 6 Sonatas (*Bärenreiter*); Concerto in D minor (Vol. 7/1 (*Ricordi*); Concerto in F (Vol. 7/2) (*Ricordi*); Concerto in A minor (*Schott*); Pastorale from Op. 13/4 (*Nagel*)

VOGT, G. (or VOIGT) (18/19): works include Solos de Concert (*Costallat*)

VOLKART-SCHLAGER, K.: Zwei Kleine Sonatinen (*Müller*)

VOORMOLEN, A. (20): Pastorale (*Donemus*)

WACHS, P. (19/20): Danse Bretonne (*Hamelle*)

WANHALL, J. (18/19): *see under* VANHALL

WESLY, E.: Rêverie d'automne (*Gaudet*)

WENNIG, H. (20): O Élegie (*Schuberth*)

WEINBERGER, J. (20): Sonatine (*Fischer*)

WEINZWEIG, J.: O Divertimento 2 (*Boosey*)

WIBLÉ, M. (20): Intermède and Rondo Varié (*Henn*)

WIERNSBERGER: En Nacelle (*Delrieu*)

WILDER, A. (20): Concerto (*A.M.P.*)

WILDSCHUT, C.: Sonatinas 1 and 2 (*Donemus*)

WILKINSON, P. (20): Suite (*Novello*)

WITT, F. (18/19): Suite in F major (*Bärenreiter*)

WOLF-FERRARI, E. (19/20): Op. 15 Idillio Concertino in A (*Ricordi*)

WOHLGEMUTH: O Concertino (*Peters*)

WOLPERT, F. A. (20): Op. 25 O Banchette Musicale 1 (*Breitkopf*)

WORDSWORTH, W. (20): Op. 57 Theme and Variations (*Lengnick*)

ZIMMERMANN, B. A. (20): O Concerto (*Schott*)

III.   OBOE WITH ORCHESTRA (solo and concertante)

P = Piano reduction available

ABACO, E. F. DALL' (17/18): Op. 5/5 Concerto in C (str. b. bc.) (*Sikorski*)

ALBINONI, T. (18): *P* Op. 7/3 Concerto (str. ce.) (*Boosey*); Op. 7/5 Concerto for 2 oboes (str. ce.) (*Kneusslin*); *P* Op. 7/6 Concerto (str. ce.) (*Boosey*); Op. 9/2 Concerto (str. ce.) (*Kneusslin or Suvini*); Op. 9/9 Concerto for 2 oboes (str. ce.) (*Ricordi*)

ALWYN, W. (20): *P* Concerto (str. hp.) (*Lengnick*)

ARMANDO, G. (20): *P* Op. 11 Concertino (str.) (*Schuberth*); Concerto in G minor (orch.) (*Schuberth*); O d'am Suite: (str.) (*Schuberth*)

ARNOLD, M. (20): *P* Op. 39 Concerto (str.) (*Paterson*)

ANDREAE (20): *P* Concertino (*Boosey*)

BACH, C. P. E. (18): *P* Concerto 1 in B flat (str. bc.) (*Leukhart*); *P* Concerto in E flat (str. bc.) (*Sikorski*)

BACH, J. C. (18): Concerto in F (2 h. str. bc.) (*Sikorski*)

BACH, J. S. (18): *P* Concerto in C minor o. v. (str. bc.) (*Peters*); also in D minor (*Breitkopf*); Sinfonia to Easter Oratorio (str. bc.) (*Breitkopf*); Sinfonia to Cantatas 12, 21, 156 (str. bc.) (*O.U.P.*); Suite 1 in C 2 o. b. (str.) (*Breitkopf*); Suite 4 in D 2 o. 2 tp. (timp. str.) (*Breitkopf*); Brandenburg Concerto 1, 3 o. 2 h. b. (str. bc.) (*Breitkopf*); Brandenburg Concerto 2, f. o. v. tp. (str. bc.) (*Breitkopf*)

BARLOW, W. (20): *P* The Winter's passed (str.) (*Eastman*)

BAUMANN (20): Kammerkonzert I f. o. (str.) (*Peters*)

BAYNTON, POWER (20): Pastorale and Rondo (small orch.) (*De Wolfe*)

BECHER, H.: Amourette (str.) (*Grosch*)

BELLINI (18): *P* Concerto in E minor (str.) (*Ricordi*)

BENTZON, N. V. (20): *P* Op. 75 Concerto (str.) (*Hansen*); *P* Op. 94 Triple Concerto o. c. b. (str.) (*Hansen*)

BERGHMANS, J. (20): *P* Le Labyrinthe (Tableaux Forains) (ch. orch.) (*Leduc*)

BJELINSKI, B.: Concerto (str.) (*M. Naklada*)

BODART, E.: Recit: und Aria (orch.) (*Zimmermann*); Musik für oboe (ch. orch.) (*Zimmermann*)

BOEDJIN, G. (20): Poëtische Suite (str. timp.) (*Donemus*)

BOEHM, Y. (20): *P* Concertino (*Israeli*)

BORDIER, J.: *P* Berceuse et Habanera (orch.) (*Durand*)

BORRIS, S.: Shakespeare Suite (str. opt. f and b.) (*Sirius*)

BÖRSCHEL, E.: Miniaturen (ch. orch.) (*Zimmermann*)

BOSCOVICH, A. U. (20): *P* Concerto (orch.) (*Israeli*)

BOUGHTON, R. (20): *P* Concerto 1 (orch.) (*Boosey*)

BOZZA, E. (20): *P* Fantaisie Pastorale (str. hp. perc. timp.) (*Leduc*)

BRÄUTIGAM, H. (20): *P* Fröhliche Musik f. o. (str.) (*Breitkopf*)

BROWN, C. (20): *P* Fantasie Agreste (str.) (*Eschig*)

BRUNS, V. (20): Op. 28 *P* Concerto (*Hofmeister*)

BUSH, G. (20): *P* Concerto (str.) (*Elkin*)

BUSSER, H. (19/20): Op. 84 *P* Asturias (str. hp. perc.) (*Leduc*); *P* Pièce en B♭ (str. hp.) (*Leduc*)

CASTELNUOVO-TEDESCO, M. (20): Op. 146 *P* Concerto da Camera (str., opt. 3 h. and timp.) (*Mills*)

CHERUBINI, L. (18/19): *CA P* Two Sonatas (str.) (*Sikorski*)

CIMAROSA/BENJAMIN (18): *P* Concerto (str.) (*Boosey*)

COLLINS, A. (20): Hogarth Suite (str.) (*Keith Prowse*)

CORELLI/BARBIROLLI (17/18): *P* Concerto (str.) (*Boosey*)

CRUFT, A. (20): Op. 25 *P* Concertante f. o. (str., opt. timp.) (*Mills*)

DAMASE, J. M. (20): *P* Rhapsodie (orch.) (*Lemoine*)

DELDEN, L. (20): Op. 64 Concerto 2 o. (orch.) (*Donemus*)

DIJK, J. VAN (20): *CA* Suite Pastorale o. ca. (ch. orch.) (*Donemus*)

D'INDY, V. (19/20): Op. 31 *P* Fantaisie (orch.) (*Durand*)

DITTERSDORF, D. VON (18): *P* Concerto in G (*Breitkopf*)

DONOVAN, R. F. (20): Ricercare (*Boosey*)

DRESDEN, S. (20): Concerto (str. timp. perc.) (*De Wolfe*)

DRESSEL, E. (20): *P* Concerto o. c. b. (orch.) (*Ries & Erler*)

DUBOIS, P. M. (20): *P* Double Concertino o. b. (str.) (*Leduc*)

EICHNER, E. (18): *P* Concerto in C (str.) (*O.U.P.*); *P* Concerto in B flat (str. ce.) (*Hofmeister*)

EMBORG (20): Op. 51 Concerto Grosso o. v. vc. (str. p.) (*Kistner*)

FARJEON, H. (20): Early Spring on Kithurst (ch. orch.) (*Hinrichsen*)

FASCH, J. F. (18): Concerti in D and G f. o. (str. bc.) (*Sikorski*); Double Concerto in D minor o. v. (str. bc.) (*Sikorski*)

FELDERHOF (20): Rhapsodie (str. timp. perc.) (*Donemus*)

FIALA (18/19): *CA* Concerto (str.) (*Artia*)

FILIPPUCCI, E.: *P* Elégie (str.) (*Enoch*)

FISCHER, J. C. (18): *P* Concerto in C (str.) (*Augener*) *P* Concerto in E flat (str. ce.)

FLEMMING, P. (18/19): *P* Concertino (*Schmidt*)

FOSS, L. (20): *P* Concerto (*Southern*)

FRICKER, P. R. (20): *CA P* Concertante (str.) (*Schott*)

GEMINIANI, F. (17/18): *P* Sonata 1 (ch. orch.) (*Ricordi*)

GENZMER, H. (20): *P* Chamber Concerto (str.) (*Schott*)

GIBILARO, A. (20): *P* Fantasy on Favourite Airs (str.) (*O.U.P.*)

GIRNATIS, W. (20): Capriccio (orch.) (*Sikorski*)

GLANVILLE-HICKS, P. (20): Gymnopédie 1 (str. hp.) (*A.M.P.*)

GLUCK/BENJAMIN (18): *P* Divertimento on themes of Gluck (str.) (*Boosey*)

GOEB, R.: Fantasy (str.) (*A.M.P.*)

GOLESTAN, S.: *P* Elégie et Danse Rustique (*Durand*)

GOOSSENS, E. (20): *P* Concerto (orch.) (*Leduc*); Op. 65 *CA* Concert Piece o./ca. 2 hp. (orch.) (*Mills*)

GRAUN, J. G. (18): *P* Concerto in C minor (str. ce.) (*Sikorski*)

GRAUPNER (18): Concerto in F minor (str. bc.) (*Nagel*)

GROOT, C. DE (20): Concertino Champêtre (orch.) (*Donemus*); Concerto for 2 o. (orch.) (*Donemus*)

HALL, R. (20): Three Idylls (str.) (*Hinrichsen*)

HANDEL, G. F. (18): *P* Concerto Grosso 8 in B♮ (str. ce.) (*Breitkopf*); *P* Concerto Grosso 9 in B♮ (str. ce.) (*Breitkopf*); *P* Concerto Grosso 10 in G minor (str. ce.) (*Breitkopf*); Concerto in E flat (str. ce.) (*Hinrichsen*); Op. 3 Concerti Grossi 2 o. (str. ce.) (*Eulenberg*)

HANNEMANN: Concerto da Camera in D (orch.) (*Kistner*)

HANSON, H. (20): Op. 38 Pastorale (str. hp.) (*Fischer*)

HAYDN, J. (18): *P* Sinfonia Concertante o. b. v. vc. (orch.) (*Breitkopf*); (attributed to) *P* Oboe Concerto in C (orch.) (*Breitkopf or O.U.P.*)

HEINICHEN, J. D. (17/18): Concerto in G (str.) (*Vieweg*)

HEMEL, O. VAN (20): Concerto (str. timp. cel.) (*Donemus*)

HIDAS, F. (20): *P* Concerto in D (orch.) (*Kultura*)

HÖFFER, P. (20): Op. 45 *P* Concerto (str.) (*Kistner*)

HOLBROOKE, J. (19/20): Quadruple Concerto f. o. c. b. (orch.) (*De Wolfe*)

HOLST, G. (19/20): *P* Fugal Concerto f. o. (str.) (*Novello*)

HONEGGER, A. (20): *CA P* Concerto da camera f. ca. (str.) (*Salabert*)

IBERT, J. (20): *P* Escales No. 2 (orch.) (*Leduc*); *P* Symphonie Concertante (str.) (*Leduc*)

INDY, *see under* D'INDY

JACOB, G. (20): *P* Concerti 1 and 2 (str.) (*Williams*); *CA P* Rhapsody (str.) (*Williams*)

KALLIWODA, J. W. (19): *P* Concerto (*Schott*)

KENNAWAY, L.: *P* Interupted Serenade (str.) (*Hinrichsen*)

KOETSIER, J. (20): Op. 14 Concertino (str. hp.) (*Donemus*); Siciliano e Rondino 2 o. (str. hp.) (*Donemus*); Op. 15/1 *CA* Vision Pastorale (str.) (*Donemus*)

KOHS, E. (20): Legend (str.) (*A.M.P.*)

KORN, P. J. (20): Op. 14 *P* Rhapsody (str.) (*Simrock*)

KROL, B.: Op. 15 *CA* Concerto Grosso o. ca. b. (str. 2 tp.) (*Böte & Bock*)

KROMMER (KRAMÁŘ), F. (18/19): Op. 52 *P* Concerto in F (*Artia*)

LAMPERSBERG, G.: Musik (orch.) (*Universal*)

LAMY, F.: *P* Rustique (str. hp. timp.) (*Leduc*)

LARSSON, L. E. (20): Op. 45/2 *P* Concertino (*Gehrmans*)

LE BOUCHER, M.: *P* Fantaisie Concertante (orch.) (*Leduc*)

LECLAIR, J. M. (18): Op. 7/3 *P* Concerto in C (*Leukhart*)

LIER, B. VAN (20): Concertante v. o. (str. p. perc.) (*Donemus*)

LUND, E.: *P* Pièce de Concert (*Böte & Bock*)

LUTYENS, E. (20): Op. 8/6 Concerto Grosso o. hp. (str.) (*Chester*)

MAASZ, G. (20) *P* Concertino (str.) (*Sikorski*)

MACONCHY, E. (20): Concerto o. b. (str.) (*Lengnick*)

MACMAHON, D. (20): *P* Concerto (str.) (*Goodwin & Tabb*); *P* Northumbrian Suite (str.) (*Elkin*)

MALIPIERO, R. (20): *P* Sonata for Oboe (str.) (*Suvini*)

MARCELLO, B. (18): *P* Concerto in C minor (str. ce.) (*De Wolfe or Forberg or Zanibon*)

MARECZEK, F.: *CA* Sommerabend am Berg (ch. orch.) (*Zimmermann*)

MARTINU, B. (20): Concerto (orch.) (*Eschig*)

MATĚJ, J.: *P* Sonata da Camera (orch.) (*Artia*)

MILDE-MEISSNER, H.: Capriccietto (ch. orch.) (*Sikorski*)

MILHAUD, D. (20): *P* Concerto (orch.) (*Heugel*)

MILWID/KRENZ (18): *P* Sinfonia Concertante (orch.) (*Moeck*)

MOLIQUE, B. (19): *P* Concertino in G (orch.) (*Breitkopf*)

MOREAU: *P* Pastorale (str. perc.) (*Leduc*)

MOZART, L. (18) (? arr.): Concerto (orch. bc.) (*Sikorski*)

MOZART, W. A. (18): K. 314 *P* Concerto in C (str. 2 o. 2 h.) (*Boosey*); K. 293 Concerto in F (short fragment: score only) (*Breitkopf*); *P* Symphony Concertante o. c. b. h. (orch.) (*Breitkopf*); K. anh. 2/94 *CA* Adagio (str. quartet) (*Kasparek*)

MÜCKENBERGER, H.: *P* Der Schäfer und die Schäferin o. b. (orch.) (*Schmidt*)

MURGIER, J. (20): *P* Concerto (orch.) (*Lemoine*)

NEMIROFF, I. (20): *P* Concerto (orch.) (*McGinnis*)

NOEL-GALLON: Concerto o. c. b. (str. timp.) (*Leduc*)

NOVAK, J. (19/20): *P* Concerto (orch.) (*Artia*)

NUSSIO, O. (20): Concerto (ch. orch.) (*Boosey*)

PAINTER, P. (20): *P* Little Pastorale (orch.) (*Fischer*)

PAUER, J. (20): *P* Concerto (orch.) (*Cesky Hudebni*)

PEDROLLO, A. (20): *P* Concertino (str.) (*Zanibon*)

PERGOLESI/BARBIROLLI (18): *P* Concerto on themes of Pergolesi (str.) (*O.U.P.*)

PERPIGNAN, F.: Souvenirs d'automne o. b. (str.) (*Enoch*)

PIERNÉ, G. (20): Pièce en sol mineur (str. timp.) (*Leduc*)

PISK, P. (20): *P* Shanty Boy (str.) (*A.M.P.*)

PISTON, W. (20): *CA* Fantasy ca. hp. (str.) (*A.M.P.*)

PLICHTA, J. (20): Scherzino (orch.) (*Continentale*)

POOT, M. (20): *P* Capriccio (orch.) (*Cebedem*)

PRIKRYL, M. (20): Detska Polka Jana 2 o. (ch. orch.) (*Kudelik*)

RAWSTHORNE, A. (20): *P* Concerto (str.) (*O.U.P.*)

RIETZ (19): *P* Konzertstück (*Breitkopf*)

RICHTER, F. X. (18): Concerto in F (str. ce.) (*Kneusslin*)

RIETI, V.: Concerto wind quintet, (orch.) (*Universal*)

ROBINSON, L. (20): *P* Concerto (str.) (*Hinrichsen*)

ROCHE, G.: Ballade (str.) (*Enoch*)

ROMAN, J. H. (18): *P* Partita in C minor (str. ce.) (*Gehrmans*); Concerto in B flat (str. ce.) (*Skanton*); Concerto for O d'am (score only) (*Akademie Lib.*)

ROPARTZ, G.: Pastorale et danse (orch.) (*Enoch*)

ROSETTI, A.: Concerto (*Breitkopf*, not for sale)

ROWLEY, A. (20): Country Idylls (*Boosey*)

SAEVERUD, H. (20): Op. 14/7 Rondo Amoroso o. b. (str.) (*Norsk*)

SAINTON, P. (20): Serenade Fantasque (str.) (*Chester*)

SALIERI, A. (18/19): *P* Concerto in C (f. o. orch.) (*Doblinger*); Triple Concerto in D o. v. vc. (orch.) (*Sikorski*)

SAVELIEV, B. (20): Concerto (orch.) (*Russian S.P.H.*)

SCARLATTI/BRYAN (18): *P* Concerto 1 (str.) (*Chester*)

SCHAEFERS, A. (20): Op. 20 *P* Concerto (orch.) (*Böte & Bock*)

SCHNEIDER ('Signor') (18): Concerto in D (str. bc.) (*Sikorski*)

SCHOECK, O. (20): *CA* Serenade o. ca. (orch.) (*Breitkopf*)

SCHROEDER, H.: Op. 34 *P* Concerto (*Müller*)

SCHWENCKE, C. G. F. (18/19): *P* Concerto in C (str. ce.) (*Hofmeister*)

SEHLBACH, E. (20): Op. 58 Concertino (orch.) (*Möseler*)

SEIDL, J. (20): Concerto (*Artia*)

SOMER, L.: Divertimento Concertante f. o. c. hp. (str.) (*Donemus*)

STAMITZ, C. (18): *P* Concerto in C minor (str. bc.) (*Sikorski*)

STANLEY/DUCK (18): Concerto (str.) (*F.D. & H.*)

STEIN, E. D.: *P* Concerto (*Schmidt*)

STÖLZEL, G. H. (18): *P* Concerto in D (str. bc.) (*Sikorski*); Double Concerto in F o. v. (str. bc.) (*Sikorski*)

STRATEGIER, H. (20): Drie Stukken (str.) (*Donemus*)

STRAUSS, R. (19/20): *P* Concerto (orch.) (*Boosey*)

TELEMANN, G. P. (17/18): *P* Concerto in F minor (str. bc.) (*Peters*); *P* Concerto in E minor (str. bc.) (*Sikorski*); *P* Concerto in D minor (str. bc.) (*Sikorski*); *P* Concerto in C minor (str. bc.) (*Schott*); Overture in C major (str. bc.) (*Sikorski*); *O d'am* Triple Concerto f. o. d'am, va. d'am. (str. bc.) (*Peters*); Suite: Musique de Table 2 o. (str. bc.) (*Breitkopf*); *P O d'am* Concerto in G (o. d'am. str.) (*Sikorski* or *Hinnenthal*); Overture (Suite) in E minor (str. bc.) (*Sikorski*); Concerto Grosso in G minor 2 o. (str. bc.) (*Sikorski*); Overture in E minor 2 o. (str. bc. b.) (*Sikorski*); Concerto (alla Francese) in C 2 o. (str. bc.) (*Sikorski*)

TOMASI, H. (20): *P* Concerto (str., opt. p.) (*Leduc*); *P* Danse Agreste (ch. orch.) (*Leduc*); Divertimento Corsica o. c. b. (str. opt., hp.) (*Leduc*)

VALENTINI, G. (17/18): Concerto 3 in C o. v. concertante, (str. ce.) (*Ricordi*)

VANHALL/TAUSKY (18/19): *P* Concerto (str.) (*O.U.P.*)

VAUGHAN WILLIAMS, R. (19/20): *P* Concerto (str.) (*O.U.P.*)

VERNON, ASHLEY (20): *P* Rhapsodie (str.) (*Elkan Vogel*)

VIVALDI, A. (17/18): Many concerti for Oboe; others for 2 oboes, and for various combinations of solo and concertante instruments (str. ce.) (*Ricordi*)

VOGEL, J. C.: Konzertante Sinfonie in C o. b. (orch.) (*Leukhart*)

VOORMOLEN, A. (20): Concerto (str. timp.) (*Donemus*); Concerto 2 o. (str. timp.) (*Donemus*)

VRANICKY, P.: Concerto in C f. o. (orch.) (*Artia*)

WARNER, T.: Four Caprices f. o. c. (str.) (*Breitkopf*)

WEINZWEIG, J.: *P* Divertimento 2 (*Boosey*)

WENNIG, H.: *P* Elegie (*Schuberth*)

H

WHETTAM, G. (20): Concertino (str.) (*De Wolfe*); *O d'am* Serenade 2 o. d'am. (ch. orch.) (*De Wolfe*)
WILDER, A.: *P* Concerto (str. perc.) (*A.M.P.*)
WOHLGEMUTH: *P* Concertino (str.) (*Peters*)
WOLF-FERRARI, E. (19/20): *P* Idillio Concertino (str. horns) (*Ricordi*); Op. 34 *CA* Kleines Konzert (str. 2 h.) (*Leukhart*)
WOLPERT, F. A. (20): Op. 25 *P* Banchette Musicale 1 (str.) (*Breitkopf*)
WOOLDRIDGE, J. (20): Concerto (str. 2 h. hp.) (*De Wolfe*)
ZIMMERMANN, B. A. (20): *P* Concerto (ch. orch.) (*Schott*)
ZIPOLI, D. (17/18): Canzone (*Universal*)

IV (I) DUETS AND TRIOS: OBOES AND COR ANGLAIS

ARDEVOL, L. (20): 4th Sonata (2 o. ca.) (*Southern*)
BACH, C. P. E. (18): Two Duos (2 o.) (*Mercury*)
BADINGS, H. (20): Trio 4a (2 o. ca.) (*Donemus*)
BEETHOVEN, L. VAN (18/19): Op. 87 Trio in C (2 o. ca.) (*Boosey* or *Breitkopf*); Variations on 'Reich mir die Hand' (Mozart) (2 o. ca.) (*Breitkopf*)
BLAVET, M. (18): Duets (2 o.) (*McGinnis*)
BOISMORTIER, J. B. DE (18): Op. 7 6 Sonatas (3 o.) (*Schott*)
CADOW (20): Kleine Suite (2 o. ca.) (*Grosch*)
CARION, F. (20): Trio (2 o. ca.) (*Brogneaux*)
CHÉDEVILLE, N. DE (17/18): 2 Pastoral Sonatas (2 o.) (*Nagel*); Six Suites (2 o.) (*Bärenreiter*)
COUPERIN, F. (18): Suite 1 (2 o.) (*Presser*)
DRESDEN, S. (19/20): Klein Trio (2 o. ca.) (*De Wolfe*)
DOBRONIC, A. (19/20): Pastorale (o. ca.) (*Schott*)
FERLING (19): 3 Duos Concertante (2 o.) (*Peters*)
GOETHE, A.: Trio (2 o. ca.) (*Barock*)
JACOB, G. (20): 2 Pieces (2 o. ca.) (*Williams*)
KAZACSAY, T.: Op. 113 Two Duets (o. ca.) (*Kultura*)
LAHUSEN (20): Kleine Pfeifermusik (2 o.) (*Breitkopf*)
LUFT, J. H. (19): Op. 11 24 Etudes in Duet Form (2 o.) (*Fischer*)
MAGANINI, Q. E. (20): Troubadours (2 o. ca.) (*Musicus*)
MIGOT, G. (20): Pastorale (2 o.) (*Leduc*)
MOEVS, R.: Duo (o. ca.) (*Eschig*)
MOSER, F. J. (20): Op. 38 Trio in C (2 o. ca.) (*Bosworth*)
RHYS, S. (20): Inventions (2 o.) (*O.U.P.*)
SELLNER (19): Duos (2 o.) (*Costallat*)
TELEMANN (18): Works include Sonatas and Canons for 2 Treble Instruments (2 o.) (*Schott*)
VALENTINE (18): Four Sonatas (2 o.) (*Fischer*)
VIGNE, P. DE LA: 2 Easy Suites (2 o.) (*Ricordi*)
VOGT: Andante Religioso (2 o. ca.) (*Costallat*)

IV (2) DUETS: OBOE AND VARIOUS INSTRUMENTS

ANDRIESSEN, J. (20): Aulos (f. o.) (*Donemus*)
ARUTYNYAN: 3 Duets (o. b.) (*Russian S.P.H.*)
BALBO, G.: Three etchings (o. c.) (*Omega*)
BAUER, M. (20): Op. 25 Duo (o. c.) (*Peters*); Improvisation and Pastorale (*E.C.I.C.*)
BERGER, A. (20): Duo (o. c.) (*Peters*)
FIALA (18/19): Duo Concertante (o. b.) (*Schmidt*)
GENZMER, H. (20): Sonata in F sharp minor (f. o.) (*Schott*)
GINASTERA (20): Duet (f. o.) (*Presser*)
GROOT, COR DE (20): Serenade (o. b.) (*Donemus*)
HEINICHEN, J. Sonata in C minor (o. b. or vc)
HOFFDING, F. (20): Op. 10 Dialoger (*Skandinavisk*)
HONEGGER, A. (20): Prelude (No. 1 of 3 Contreponts) (o. vc.) (*Hansen*)
HOVHANESS, A.: Prelude and Fugue (o. b.) (*Whitney*); Suite (ca. b.) (*Blake*)
JACOB, G. (20): Three Inventions (f. o.) (*Williams*)
KLERK, A. DE (20): Sarabande and Sicilienne (f. o.) (*Heuwekemeyer*)
KUNERT, K.: Op. 15 Sonata (f. o.) (*Grosch*)
LACOMBE, P. (19/20): Passepied (o. b. or vc.) (*Durand*)
LAHUSEN, C.: Kleine Pfeifermusik (o. c.) (*Breitkopf*)
MAGANINI, Q. E. (20): Berger et Bergère (f. o.) (*Fischer*); Air and Double (o. c.) (*Fischer*); Two Pastorales (o. b.) (*Fischer*)
NAUMANN, J. G. (18): Duet in B flat (o. b.) (*Sikorski*)
NEMIROFF, I. (20): Four Treble Suite (f. o.) (*McGinnis*)
PHILLIPS, G. (20): Suite in B flat (c. o.) (*Schott*)
RAPHAEL, G. (20): Op. 65/2 Sonatine (o. h.) (*Breitkopf*)
RIEGGER, W. (20): Op. 35 Duos (f. o.) (*Presser*)
RUST, F. W.: Sonata (o. hp. or p.) (*Pro Musica*)
SANGIORGI, A. (20): Duo Sonata (o. b.) (*Forlivesi*)
SEHLBACH, E. (20): Op. 53/2 Duet (f. o.) (*Möseler*)
SMIT, L. (20): Suite (o. vc.) (*Donemus*)
TOMASI, H. (20): Le Tombeau de Mireille (o. tamb. or p.) (*Leduc*)
VILLA-LOBOS, H. (20): Duo (o. b.) (*Eschig*)
VOSS, F. (20): Notturno (o. hp.) (*Breitkopf*)
WETZGER: Forward and Backward (2 Musical Jokes) (v. o.) (*Schmidt*)
WIENER: Op. 2 Duo (f. ca.) (*Universal*)

IV (3) TRIOS WITHOUT KEYBOARD INSTRUMENT
(*see also* IV (9))
(oboe, clarinet, and bassoon unless otherwise stated)

ADDISON, J. (20): Trio (*Williams*)
AMBERG, J. (20): Suite (f. o. c.) (*Nordiska*)
ANDRIESSEN, J. (20): Trio 4 (f. o. b.) (*Donemus*)

ARDEVOL, J. (20): 1st Sonata (o. c. vc.) (*Southern*)
ARNOLD, M. (20): Divertimento (f. o. c.) (*Paterson*)
ARRIEU, C. (20): Trio (*Amphion*)
AURIC, G. (20): Trio (*Oiseau-Lyre*)
BADEN, C. (20) Trio (f. o. c.) (*Lyche*)
BADINGS, H. (20): Trio (*Donemus*)
BALORRE: Trio (o. va. vc.) (*Hamelle*)
BARRAUD, H. (20): Trio (*Oiseau-Lyre*)
BAUERFEIND, H.: Heitere Musik (o. c. b. or o. va. vc.) (*Doblinger*)
BAUMANN, H.: Divertimento (*Sikorski*)
BELINFANTE, D. (20): Trio (f. o. b.) (*Donemus*)
BENTZON, J. (20): Racconte 3 (*Skandinavisk*); Op. 7 Sonatina
    (*Skandinavisk*)
BERTONVILLE, G.: Prelude and Fugue (*Cebedem*)
BLOMDAHL, K. B.: Trio (*F.S.T.*)
BLUMENTHAL: Trio (f. o. b.) (*Peters*)
BONNEAU: Trois Vieilles Chansons de Noël (o., ca. or c., b.) (*Leduc*)
BOVÉ, J. H.: Petit Trio (*Fischer*)
BORNEFELD, H.: Neue Musik (f. o. c.) (*Bärenreiter*)
BOUTRY (20): Divertissement (*Leduc*)
BOZZA, E. (20): Suite Brève en Trio (*Leduc*)
BRINK-POTHUIS, A. (20): Op. 4 and 33 Trios 1 and 2 (*Donemus*)
BULLING, B. (20): Suite (*Grosch*)
BURKHARD, W. (20): Op. 76 Canzona (f. o. vc.) (*Bärenreiter*)
BUTTERWORTH, A. (20): Trio (*Hinrichsen*)
CANTELOUBE, J. (19/20): Rustiques (*Oiseau-Lyre*)
CARION, F.: Op. 19 Bagatelles (f. o. c.) (*Brogneaux*)
CHEMIN-PETIT, H. (20): Trio in Olden Style (*Lienau*)
CHIAFFARELLI, A.: Serenade (f. o. c.) (*Alfred*)
CLEMENTI, A.: works include Tre Piccoli Pezzi (f. o. c.) (*Suvini*)
CONSTANT, M. (20): Trio (*Chester*)
DAHLHOFF, W.: Drei Sätze (f. o. c.) (*Schmidt*); Idyll Pan and Nymph
    (f. o., hp. or p.) (*Schmidt*)
DANIEL-LESURE (20): Suite (*Oiseau-Lyre*)
DANIELS, M. (20): Three Observations (*Fischer*)
DEFOSSEZ, R. (20): Trio (*Cebedem*)
DRAEGER-GLASENAPP-GÖRNER: Trio (f. o. c.) (*Hofmeister*)
DUBOIS, P. M. (20): Trio d'Anches (*Leduc*)
ESCHER, R. (20): Op. 4 Trio d'Anches (*Donemus*)
ETLER: Sonata (o. c. va.) (*Valley*)
FASCH, J. F. (18): Sonata in F (2 o. b.) (*Sikorski*)
FAVRE, G. (20): Gouaches (*Durand*)
FELDERHOF, J. (20): Rondo (*Donemus*); Thema Mit Variaties
    (*Donemus*)

FELDMAN, L. (20): Suita (f. o. c.) (*Rumanian S.P.H.*)

FERROUD, P. O. (20): Trio in E (*Durand*)

FLÉGIER, A. (19/20): Trio (*Gallet*)

FLOTHUIS, M. (20): Op. 11 Nocturne (f. o. c.) (*Chester*)

FÔRET, F.: Suite en trio (*Costallat*)

FORTNER, W. (20): Serenade (f. o. b.) (*Schott*)

FRANCAIX, J. (20): Divertissement (*Eschig*)

FRANCK, M.: Trio (*Mus. Transatlantija*)

FRID, G. (20): *CA* 7 Pieces (f. ca. b.) (*Donemus*)

GALLON, N.: Suite en trio (*Selmer*)

GENNARO, M. (20): Trio (f. o. c.) (*Evette*)

GERAEDTS, J. (20): Divertimenti 1 and 2 (*Donemus*); Divertimento 2 (*Donemus*)

GOEB, R. (20): Suite (f. o. c.) (*Southern*)

GOLESTAN, S. (19/20): Petite Suite Bucolique (*Durand*)

GOUÈ, E.: 3 Pieces for Trio (*Schneider*)

GÖRNER, H. G. (20): Op. 24 Trio (f. o. c.) (*Hofmeister*)

GRABNER, H.: Trio (*Kistner*)

GRAUN, K. H. (18): *O d'am* Trios 1 and 2 in D and E (o d'am. h. b.) *McGinnis*)

GRAUPNER, J. C. (18): Suite in F (f. 2 o.) (*Peters*)

GRIEND, K. VAN DE (20): Trio (*Donemus*)

HANDEL, G. F. (18): Rigaudon, Bourrée, and March (2 o. b. opt. sidedrum) (*Musica Rara*)

HARCOURT, D'.: Rapsodie Peruvienne (*Lemoine*)

HEMEL, O. VAN (20): Trio (f. o. b.) (*Donemus*)

HERMANS, N. (20): Op. 2 Divertimento Piccolo (*Donemus*)

HÖFFER, P. (20): Kleine Suite (*Sikorski*); Theme with Variations (*Sikorski*)

HOLST, G. (19/20): Terzetto (f. o. va.) (*Chester*)

HUGUENIN: Op. 30 and 31 2 Trios (o. c. b.) (*Southern*)

IBERT, J. (20): Cinq Pièces en Trio (*Oiseau-Lyre*)

IKONOMOV, B.: Trio (*Oiseau-Lyre*)

IPPOLITOV-IVANOV: 2 Kirghiz Songs (*Mercury*)

JACOBSOHN, G. (20): Adagio and Allegro (o. c. h.) (*Israeli*)

JELINEK, H. (20): Op. 15/7 *CA* Sonatina a Tre (o. ca. b.) (*Universal*)

JEMNITZ, A. (20): Op. 19 Trio (f. o. c.) (*Zimmerman*)

JOHANSON, S. E.: Lyric Suite (*F.S.T.*)

JOLIVET, A. (20): Pastorales de Noël (f. o. b.) (*Heugel*)

JONGEN, L. (20): Trio (*Southern*)

JUON, P. (19/20): Op. 73 Arabesques (*Schott*)

KARG-ELERT, S. (19/20): Op. 49/1 *CA* Trio in D minor (o. ca. c.) (*Hofmeister*)

KELKEL, M.: Divertimento (*Ricordi*)

KLEIN, R. R.: Serenade (*Hinrichsofen*)
KOECHLIN, C. H. (19/20) Trio (*Marbot*)
KOETSIER, J. (20): Op. 16/2 6 Bagatellen (*Donemus*)
KONIETZNY, H.: Kleine Kammermusik 2 (*Modern*)
KONSTANTINOFF: Trio (*De Wolfe*)
KREJČÍ, I. (20): Trio Divertimento (*Artia*)
KRIENS, C. (20): Ronde des Lutins (f. o. c.) (*Fischer*)
KUBIZEK, A.: 4 Pieces (o. c. bass c.) (*Breitkopf*)
KUKUCK, F.: Kammermusik (f. o. vg.) (*Möseler*)
KURTZBACH: Trio (*Peters*)
LEGLEY, V. (20): Op. 11 Trio (*Cebedem*)
LEWIN, G. (20): Scherzola (*New Wind*)
LOYON, E.: Scherzo (*Costallat*)
MACHAUT, G. DE.: Double Hoquet pour 3 instr. de Vent (*Oiseau-Lyre*)
MAEGAARD, J.: Trio (*Larsen*)
MAESSEN, A. (20): Cassation (*Donemus*)
MAGANINI, Q. E. (20): Geographs 1, 2, 3 (*Fischer*)
MAROS, R. (20): Serenade (*Kultura*)
MARTELLI, H. (20): Op. 45 Trio (*Costallat*)
MARTINON, J. (20): Sonatine 4 (*Costallat*)
MARTINU, B. (20): Four Madrigals (*Eschig*)
MELKIKH, D.: Op. 17 Trio (*Universal*)
MENGELBERG, K. (20): Trio (f. o. b.) (*Donemus*)
MEULEMANS, A.: Trio (*Brogneaux*)
MIGOT, G. (20): Thrène (*Leduc*); Trio (*Leduc*)
MILHAUD, D. (20): Suite d'Après Corette (*Oiseau-Lyre*); Pastorale (*Chant du Monde*)
MOSËR, R.: Op. 51/1 Divertimento (f. o. c.) (*Steingräber*)
MULDER, E. W. (20): Fuga VII (ars Contrepunctica) (f. o. b.) (*Donemus*)
MULDER, H.: *CA* Trio (f. ca. b.) (*Donemus*)
NILSSON, B. (20): 20 Gruppen (pic. o. c.) (*Universal*)
OLSEN, S. (20): Op. 10 Suite (f. o. c.) (*Lyche*)
ORBAN, M.: Prélude, Pastorale and Divertissement (*Durand*)
PELEMANS, W.: Trio 2 (*Maurer*)
PESCETTI, G. B.: Presto (f. o. b.) (*Musicus*)
PFEIFFER, G. (19): Musette (*Rouart-Maurer*)
PHILLIPS, G. (20): Pastorale (f. o. c.) (*Hinrichsen*)
PIERNÉ, P. (20): Bucolique Var. (*Costallat*)
POOT, M. (20): Ballade (*Eschig*); Divertimento (*Eschig*)
PRAAG, H. VAN (20): Fantasia a Tre (f. o. b.) (*Donemus*)
RATHAUS, K.: Gavotte Classique (f. o. b.) (*Boosey*)
RIVIER, J. (20): Suite (*Marbot*)
RÖNTGEN, J. (19/20): Op. 86 Trio (f. o. b.) (*Alsbach*)

ROPARTZ, G.: Entrata and Scherzetto (*Salabert*)
ROSSEAU, N. (20): Op. 53 3 Jouets (*Cebedem*)
SAUGUET, H. (20): Trio (*Oiseau-Lyre*)
SAVNIK, V.: Fughetta (f. o. b.) (*M. Naklada*)
SCHISKE, K.: Op. 41 Trio Sonata (*Döblinger*)
SCHLEMM, G. A.: Trio (*Grosch*)
SCHMITT, C. (20): Trio (*Cebedem*)
SCHOEMAKER, M. (20): Suite Champêtre (*Cebedem*)
SCHULOFF, E. (20): Divertissement (*Schott*)
SENSTIUS, K.: Op. 36 Serenade (o. va. b.) (*Larsen*)
SIEGL, O. (20): Op. 145 Trifolium (f. o. va.) (*Hofmeister*)
SLAVICKY (20): Trio (*Artia*)
SMAJLOVIČ, A.: Trio (*M. Naklada*)
SMIT SIBINGS, T. H. (20): Plain Music (f. o. c.) (*Donemus*)
SPISAK, M. (20): Sonatine (*Moeck*)
STIEBER, H.: Spielmusik 1 (2 o. b.) (*Hofmeister*)
SURINACH, C. (20): Tientos (o. hp. timp.) (*Union Musical*)
SZALOWSKI, A. (20): Trio Divertimento (*Chester*)
TAK, P. C.: Präludium, Choral and Fugue (*Donemus*)
TANSMAN, A. (20): Suite pour Trio d'Anches (*Eschig*)
THIRIET, M.: Suite (*Marbot*)
THOMPSON, R. (20): Suite (o. c. va.) (*Schirmer*)
TOMASI, H. (20): Concert Champêtre (*Lemoine*)
TRUDIČ, B.: Trio (*M. Naklada*)
VELLONES, P.: Op. 94 Trio (f. o. hp.) (*Durand*)
VEREMANS, M.: Trio 1 (*Metropolis*)
VERESS, S.: Sonatina (*Suvini*)
VERHAAR, A. (20): Op. 38 Trio (f. o. c.) (*Donemus*)
VIECENZ, F.: Terzetto (2 o. h.) (*Hofmeister*)
VILLA-LOBOS, H. (20): Trio (*Eschig*)
VINÉE, A. (19/20): *CA* Trio Serenade (f. ca. hp., or p.) (*Durdilly*)
VOLBACH, F.: Op. 24 Trio (*Breitkopf*)
WAILLY, P. DE (19/20): Aubade (f. o. c.) (*Rouart*)
WALKER, R. (20): Bagatelle (f. o. c.) (*A.M.P.*)
WAGNER-REGENY: Suite (*Universal*)
WEBER, A.: Trio d'Anches (*Leduc*)
WEBER, E. VON: Trio (o. va. b.) (*Simrock*)
WENNIG, H.: Volksliedsätze (*Hofmeister*)
WHETTAM, G. (20): Divertimento 1 (*De Wolfe*)
WIENER, K. (20): Op. 20 *CA* Three Pieces (f. ca. c.) (*Universal*)
WIJDEVELD, W. (20): Op. 64 Trio (f. o. b.) (*Donemus*)
WILDBERGER, J.: Trio (*Modern*)
WISSMER, P. (20): Serenade (*Costallat*)
WOESTIJNE, D. VAN DE: Divertimento (*Cebedem*)

ZAGWIJN, H. (20): Trios 1 and 2 (f. o. c.) (*Donemus*); Suite (2 o. heck.) (*Donemus*)

ZBINDEN, J. F. (20): Op. 12 Trio d'Anches (*Lemoine*)

ZIMMERMANN, H. (20): Trios 1 and 2 (o. b. vc.) (*Schmidt*)

ZNIDAR, J. (20): Fuga in Scherzando (*M. Naklada*)

IV (4) TRIOS WITH KEYBOARD INSTRUMENT

ADDISON, J. (20): Trio (f. o. p.) (*Augener*)

AGNEL, E.: Op. 1 Pastorale (ca. b. p.) (*Costallat*); Op. 2 Trio (o.b. p.) (*Costallat*)

ANDRIESSEN, H. (20): Theme mit Variaties (f. o. p.) (*Donemus*)

ANDRIESSEN, J. (20): Trio 1 (f. o. p.) (*Donemus*)

BACH, J. C.: Divertimento (f. o. p.) (*Andraud*)

BACH, J. S. (18): *O* Concerto in C Minor (o. v. p.) (*Peters*); Canonic Trio (f. o. p.) (*McGinnis*)

BECKERATH, A. VON: Sonatine (2 o. p.) (*Moeck*)

BLANC, A.: Op. 14 Trio (o. b. p.) (*Costallat*)

BODINUS, S. (18): Trio Sonata (2 o. bc.) (*Vieweg*)

BOEDIJN, G. (20): Op. 87 Folklörische Suite (f. o. p.) (*Donemus*)

BOISMORTIER, J. DE (18): Concerto: A minor (2 o. p.) (*Ricordi*); Concerto in C (f. o. bc.) (*Ricordi*)

BOWEN, Y. (20): Ballade (o. h. p.) (*De Wolfe*)

BURKHARD, W. (20): Op. 76 Canzona (f. o. p.) (*Bärenreiter*)

BUSH, G. (20): Trio (o. b. p.) (*Novello*)

CIMA, G. P. (16/17): Sonata 3 (from Drei Sonaten) (o. v. bc.) (*Sikorski*)

CIMAROSA, D. (18): Concerto in G (f. o. p.) (*Andraud*)

CRUFT, A. (20): Op. 25 *O* Concertante (f. o. p.) (*Mills*)

DAHLHOFF, W.: Idyll: Pan and Nymph (f. o. p. or hp.) (*Schmidt*)

DESTENAY, E. (20): Op. 27 Trio (o. c. p.) (*Hamelle*)

DIAMOND, D. (20): Partita (o. b. p.) (*Southern*)

DIJK, J. VAN (20): Canzona alla Capriccio (o. b. p.) (*Donemus*)

DUBOIS, P. M. (20): *O* Double Concertino (o. b. p.) (*Leduc*)

DUBOIS, T. (19/20): Deux Pièces en Forme Canonique (o. vc. p.) (*Heugel*)

EVANS, D. MOULE: See Moule Evans

FASCH, J. F. (18): Sonata in B flat (o. v. bc.) (*Bärenreiter*); Op. 3/1 Sonata (2 o. p.) (*Nagel*); Sonata in D minor (2 o. bc.) (*Sikorski*); Canon Sonata à 3 (o. b. bc.) (*Moeck*)

FINGER, G. (18): Sonata in F (f. o. p.) (*Nagel*)

FRESCOBALDI (17): Fünf Canzone (für 2 höhe inst.) (2 o. bc.) (*Schott*)

FUX, J. J. (17/18): Sinfonia (f. o. bc.) (*Nagel*); Trio Sonata in B flat (o. v. bc.) (*Nagel*); Nürnberger Partita (f. o. ce.) (*Möseler*)

GAL, H. (20): Op. 49 Trio (o. vc. p.) (*Oesterreich*)

GALUPPI, B. (18): Trio (f. o. bc.) (*Kneusslin*); Trio Sonata in G (o. v. bc.) (*Bärenreiter*)

GODRON, H. (20): Stotiniana (o. b. p.) (*Donemus*)

GOOSSENS, E. (20): Pastorale and Harlequinade (f. o. p.) (*Leduc*)

GRAUN, J. G. (18): Trio in F (v. o. p.) (*Breitkopf*)

GRETZKY, G.: Trio Sonata in G (f. o. bc.) (*Bärenreiter*)

HAMM: Dialogue (f. o. p.) (*Fischer*)

HANDEL, G. F. (18): Trio Sonata in F (o. b. bc.) (*Breitkopf*); several Trio Sonatas (2 o. bc.) (*Bärenreiter* or *Breitkopf* or *Moeck* or *Musica Rara* or *Peters* or *Schott*)

HASSE, J. A. (18): Trio Sonata in F (o. v. bc.) (*Sikorski*)

HEINICHEN, J. D. (18): Sonata in G (f. o. p.) (*Breitkopf*); Trio (o. vg. p.) (*Doblinger*); Trio Sonata in C minor (o. v. bc.) (*Sikorski*)

HENRICH: Op. 23 Trio Suite (o. h. p.) (*Heinrichshofen*)

HERTEL, J. G. (18): Drei Partiten (o. oblig. org., or ce. bc.) (*Sikorski*)

HERZOGENBERG: Op. 61 Trio (o. h. p.) (*Peters*)

HILL, A. (19/20): Miniature Trio (o. vc. p.) (*Schirmer*)

HOLBROOKE, J. (19/20): Op. 57/1 Nocturne (o. va. p.) (*Modern Music Lib.*)

HOLST, G. (19/20): O Fugal Concerto (f. o. p.) (*Novello*)

HONEGGER, A. (20): *CA* O Concerto da Camera (f. ca. p.) (*Salabert*)

JACOB, G. (20): Trio (f. o. ce. or p.) (*O.U.P.*)

JANITSCH, J. G. (18): Op. 8 Kammersonate 'Echo' in D (f. o. ce.) (*Breitkopf*)

KAHN, R. (19/20): Serenade (o. h. or va., p.) (*Universal*)

KAUDER, H. (20): Trio (o. vc. or h. p.) (*Universal*)

KETTING, P. (20): Sonata (f. o. p.) (*Donemus*)

KOETSIER, J. (20): Op. 13/1 Little Rural Suite (f. o. p.) (*Donemus*)

KOPSCH, J. (20): Trio (o. c. p.) (*Universal*)

KOTSCHAU: 2 Divertimenti (o. va. p.) (*Zimmermann*)

LACOMBE, H. (19/20): Op. 47 Serenade (f. o. p.) (*Hamelle*)

LALLIET: Op. 22 Terzetto (o. b. p.) (*Hamelle*)

LEGLEY, V.: Op. 11 Trio (o. b. p.) (*Cebedem*)

LEIGH, W. (20): Trio (f. o. p.) (*O.U.P.*)

LILIEN, I. (20): Music for the Smiling Tomorrow (f. o. p.) (*Donemus*)

LOEFFLER (19/20): 2 Rhapsodies (o. va. p.) (*Schirmer*)

LOEILLET, J. (17/18): Op. 1/3 and 5 Trio Sonatas in G and C (r. or f., o. bc.) (*Mus. Rara*); Op. 2/2 and 6 Trio Sonatas in F and C (r. or f., o. bc.) (*Mus. Rara*)

LOEILLET, J. B. (17/18): Trio Sonatas in C and G minor (f. o. p.) (*Lemoine*); Op. 1/1 Trio Sonata in F (f. o. p.) (*Schott*)

LOTTI, A. (17/18): O d'am Trio in A (f. o. d'am. or o., bc.) (*Ricordi*)

MASSÉUS, J. (20): Intro. and Allegro (o. c. p.) (*Donemus*)

MILNE, J. (20): Scherzetto (o. b. p.) (*Chester*)

MOULE EVANS, D. (20): Suite (f. o. p.) (*Williams*)

MÜCKENBERGER, H.: Der Schäfer und die Schäferin (o. b. p.) (*Schmidt*)

OTTEN, L. (20): Musette et Pastourelle (f. o. p.) (*Donemus*)

PAISIBLE, J. (17/18): Sonata Prima (2 o. bc.) (*Moeck*)

PELEMANS, W.: Sonatas 1 and 2 (f. o. p.) (*Maurer*)

PEPUSCH, J. C. (17/18): 6 Trio Sonatas (v. or f., o. p.) (*Breitkopf*); Trio Sonata in G (f. o. ce.) (*Peters*); Sonata (o. v. ce.) (*Schott*)

PHILLIPS, G.: Pastorale (f. o. p.) (*Peters*)

PILLEVESTRE: Idylle Bretonne (2 o. p.) (*Leduc*); or (o. b. p.) (*Leduc*)

PITFIELD, T. B. (20): Trio in D minor (f. o. p.) (*Augener*); Trio in F minor (o. b. p.) (*Augener*)

PLANEL, R. (20): Andante and Scherzo (o. b. p.) (*Selmer*)

POULENC, F. (20): Trio (o. b. p.) (*Hansen*)

PROWO, P. (18): Sonatas 5 and 6 à 3 (2 o. bc.) (*Moeck*)

QUANTZ, J. J. (18): Trio in C minor (f. o. p.) (*Zimmermann*); Trio in D (o. v. ce.) (*Bärenreiter* or *Kistner* or *Ricordi*); Trio in C (f. o. p.) (*Schott*); Trio Sonata in G (2 o. bc.) (*Bärenreiter*); Trio Sonata in E minor (2 o. bc.) (*Sikorski*)

REINECKE, C. (19/20): Op. 188 Trio in A minor (o. h. p.) (*Breitkopf*)

REIZENSTEIN, F. (20): Op. 25 Trio in A (f. o. p.) (*Lengnick*)

ROBBINS, G. (20): Pastorale and Bagatelle (f. o. p.) (*U.M.P.*)

ROESGEN-CHAMPION: Pastorale (o. vc. p.) (*Senart*)

ROMAN, J. H. (18) Trio Sonata (2 o. p.) (*Nordiska*)

RUTHARDT, A. (19/20): Op. 34 Trio in G (o. v. p.) (*Kahnt*)

RUYNEMAN, D. (20): Amatarasu (Ode on a Japanese Melody) (f. o. p.) (*Donemus*); Kobune (f. o. ce.) (*Donemus*)

SALIERI, A. (18/19): O Concerto in C (f. o. p.) (*Doblinger*)

SCHUYT, N. (20) Sonata a Tre (o. b. p.) (*Donemus*)

SMYTH, E. (19/20): Two Interlinked French Folk Melodies (f. o. p.) (*O.U.P.*)

STOLZEL, G. H. (18): Trio Sonata in F minor (2 o. bc.) (*Nagel*); Trio Sonata (2 o. bc.) (*Bärenreiter*); Sonata in C minor (o. v. ce.) (*Breitkopf*); Sonata in E minor (f. o. ce.) (*Breitkopf*)

STRADELLA, A. (17): Sinfonia a Tre (2 o. bc.) (*Schott*)

TAK, P. C.: Trio (f. o. p.) (*Donemus*)

TELEMANN, G. P. (17/18): works include Trio in E minor (f. o. p.) (*Bärenreiter* or *Breitkopf* or *Nagel*); Trio in C minor (f. o. p.) (*Forberg* or *Breitkopf* or *Peters*); O d'am Trio Sonata in A (o. d'am. v. bc.) (*Sikorski*); Trio Sonata in G minor (v. o. bc.) (*Sikorski*); Trio Sonata in E♭: (O. Konzertierendes ce. bc.) (*Sikorski*); Trio Sonata in D minor (f. o. bc.) (*Sikorski*); Trio Sonata in B flat (o. v. bc.) (*Sikorski*); 2 ème Concert (f. o. p.) (*Delrieu*); Sonata in F (f. o. bc.) (*Moeck*); Sonate en Trio (o. v. bc.) (*Foetisch*); Trio Sonata in C minor (o. va. bc.) (*Sikorski*)

TOVEY, D. (19/20): *CA* Trio in D minor (v. ca. p.) (*Schott*)
TRINKHAUS, G. J. (20): Lament (o. b. p.) (*Fischer*)
VERHAAR, A. (20): Op. 18 Trio (f. o. p.) (*Donemus*)
VINÉE, A. (19/20): *CA* Trio Serenade (f. ca. p. or hp.) (*Durdilly*)
VIVALDI, A. (17/18): Trio (2 o. bc.) (*Moeck*). *Note.* The complete
    edition of works by Vivaldi is still being published. Inquiries
    should be made to *Ricordi.*
WEBER, E. Op. 27 Terzetto (o. vc. p. or org.) (*Bosworth*)
WECKERLIN, J. B. (19/20): Pastorale (f. o. p.) (*Heugel*)
WHETTAM, G. (20): Divertimento 2 (o. b. p.) (*De Wolfe*)
WHITE, F. (20): The Nymph's Complaint (o. va. p.) (*S. & B.*)
ZACHOW, F. W. (17/18): Kammertrio (o. b. bc.) (*Kistner*)
ZAGWIJN, H. (20): Pastorale and Scherzo (f. o. ce.) (*Donemus*)
ZELENKA, J. D. (17/18): Sonatas 1, 4, 5, 6 in F, G minor, F, C minor
    (2 o. bc.) (*Bärenreiter*)

IV (5) QUARTETS WITHOUT KEYBOARD INSTRUMENT
(*see also* IV (9))
(flute, oboe, clarinet, and bassoon unless otherwise stated)

ARNELL, R. (20): Cassation in 5 parts (*Hinrichsen*)
BAIRD, T. (20): Divertimento (*Moeck*)
BECHER, H.: *CA O d'am* Ansbacher Quartet (o. o. d'am. ca. heck. or
    b.) (*Grosch*)
BECKERATH, A. VON: Musik Für 4 Instrumente (o. 2 c. b.) (*Hohner*)
BERGER, A. (20): Quartet in C (*Arrow*)
BITSCH, M. (20): Divertissement (*Leduc*)
BLACHER, B. (20): Op. 38 Divertimento (*Schott*)
BOZZA, E. (20): works include Op. 42 Variants and Op. 48 Scherzo
    (*Leduc*)
BRIDGE, F. (20): Divertimento (*Boosey*)
BUTT (20): Winsome's Folly (o. c. h. c.) (*Boosey*)
BUTTING: Op. 70 *CA* Kleine Kammermusik (f. ca. v. vc.) (*Peters*)
CARTER, E.: 8 Etudes and a Fantasy (*A.M.P.*)
CHAILLEY, J. (20): Suite du 15 ème Siècle (o. b. h. tamb.) (*Leduc*)
CHAVEZ (20): Soli (o. c. tp. b.) (*Boosey*)
COX, N. (20) Minuet (*Boosey*)
DAHLHOFF, W. (20): A Dramatic Dance Scene (*Schmidt*)
DELAMARTER: Sketch Book in Eire (*Southern*)
DONOVAN (20): Quartet (*Valley*)
DURAND: Op. 62 Chaconne (f. o. c. p.) (*Presser*)
EGIDI, A.: Op. 19 Quartet (*Kultura*)
EHRENBERG, C.: Op. 40 Quartet (o. c. h. b.) (*Simrock*)
ERIKSSON, N.: Quartet (*F.Š.T.*)
ETLER, A. (20): Quartet (o. c. b. va.) (*Valley*)

FERNANDEZ: Op. 37/2 Suite in F (*A.M.P.*)

FRANCAIX, J. (20): Quartet (*Eschig*)

GENDELEV, D.: Quartet on Russian Themes (*Russian S.P.H.*)

GOEB, R.: Suite 2 (2 f. o. c.) (*Peer*)

GOEPFART, K. E.: Op. 93 Quartet (f. o. h. b.) (*Schuberth*)

GRETZKY, G.: Two Pieces (*Russian S.P.H.*)

HAYDN, JOH. M. (18): Divertimento in D (f. o. h. b.) (*Hofmeister*)

HENNEBERG, A.: Little Quartet (f. o. h. b.) (*F.S.T.*)

HOLBROOKE, J. (19/20): Serenade (*Modern Music Lib.*)

HONEGGER, A. (20): *CA* Canon sur Basse Ostinée (No. 3 of Trois Contrepoints) (pic. o. (ca.), v. vc.) (*Hansen*)

HOVHANESS, A. (20): Op. 61/5 Divertimento (o. c. h. b.) (*Peters*)

HUGUES, L.: Op. 72 and 76 2 Quartets (*Ricordi*)

HYE-KNUDSEN, J. (20): Op. 3 *CA* Quartet (f. o. (ca.) v. vc.) (*Hansen*)

JOLIVET (20): Pastorales de Noël (*Heugel*)

JONES (20): Lyric Waltz Suite (*Peters*)

JONGEN: 2 Paraphrases on Walloon Carols (*Southern*)

KOSENKO, W.: 5 LIEDER (*Russian S.P.H.*)

KRIEGER, J. P. (17/18): *CA* Partita in F (2 o. ca. b.) (*Kistner*)

KROL, B.: Op. 5 8 Spielstücke (*Pro Musica*)

KURKA, R.: Moravian Folksongs (*Weintraub*)

KROGER, J.: Partie 9 in F (2 o. ca. b.) (*Kistner*)

LAJTHA, L. (20): Quatre Hommages (*Leduc*)

LAUBER, J.: *CA* 4 Intermezzi (f. ca. c. b.) (*K.M.P.*)

LEVITIN: Suite (*Russian S.P.H.*)

LIPATTI, D. (20): Aubade (*Broude*)

LONG, N. H. (20): Scherzino (In the Aquarium) (f. o. 2 c.) (*Fischer*)

LULLY, J. B. (17): *CA* Military Marches (2 o ca. b., opt. drums) (*Mus. Rara*)

MAASZ, G. (20): Finkenschlag Variationen (*Sikorski*)

MALIPIERO, G. F. (20): Sonata a Quattro (*Universal*); Epodi e Giambi (v. o. va. b.) (*Hansen*)

MANSON, E.: Fugue (*A.M.P.*)

MAZELLIER, J.: Dix Fugues sur des Sujets Donnés (*Lemoine*)

MIELENZ, H.: *CA* Scherzo (f. ca. c. b.) (*Ries & Erler*)

MIRANDOLLE, L.: Quartet (*Leduc*)

MORTARI, V. (20): Three Old Dances (f. o. va. vc.) (*Carisch*)

MOZART, W. A. (18) (attributed to): Cassazione (o. c. h. b.) (*Andraud—Southern*)

MULDER, E. W. (20): Quartet (o. b. vc. hp.) (*Donemus*)

NEMIROFF, I. (20): Four Treble Suites (f. o. 2 c.) (*McGinnis*)

PAULSON, G.: Op. 73 Quartet (*F.S.T.*); Op. 22 Little Serenade (*E.S.T.*)

PETYREK, F.: Güte Nacht, O Welt (o. c. h. b.) (*Doblinger*)

PISK, P. (20): Little Woodwind Music (o. 2 c. b.) (*A.M.P.*)

POOT, M. (20): Petite Marche de Fête (*Cebedem*)

POZAJIC: *CA* Three Compositions (2 o. ca. b.) (*M. Naklada*)

PRAAG, H. C. VAN (20): Quartet (*Donemus*); Drie Schetsen (*Donemus*)

PROKOFIEFF, S. (20): Fleeting Moments (*Cundy*)

PROVINCIALLI, E.: Danse Villageoise (*Eschig*)

RAASTED, O. (20): Serenade (f. o. va. vc.) (*Skandinavisk*)

RAPHAEL, G. (20): Op. 61 Quartet (*Müller*)

REGNER, H.: Serenade (o. c. h. b.) (*Heinrichsofen*)

RENZI, A.: 5 Bagatelles (*De Santis*)

RIJSAGER, K. (20): Quartet (*Larsen*)

ROSSINI, G. (19): Quartet (f. or o., c. h. b.) (*Ricordi*)

RUBBRA, E. (20): Op. 106 Notturno (pic. f. o. c.) (*Lengnick*)

SABALYEV, B.: Suite (*Russian S.P.H.*)

SANDERS, R. L. (20): The Imp (o. 2 c. b. or o. 3 c.) (*Fischer*)

SAWELJEW, B. W.: Suite (*Russian S.P.H.*)

SCARMOLIN, A.: Op. 36 Scherzo (*Fischer*)

SCHAFFNER, N.: Op. 5 3 Quartets (*Boosey* (*U.S.A.*))

SCHIERBECK, P.: Capriccio (*Hansen*)

SHAW, O.: For the Gentlemen (*Mercury*)

SONTAG, W.: Quartet on Old Tunes (*Presser*)

SOURILAS, T.: Suite (o. h. vc. hp. or p.) (*Lemoine*)

STAMITZ, K. (18): Op. 8/2 Quartet in E flat (o. c. h. b.) (*Leukhart*)

TSEIGER, Y.: Suite on Esthonian Themes (f. o. c. h.) (*Russian S.P.H.*)

TUTHILL, B. (20): Divertimento (*Fischer*)

VALENTINI, G.: Quartettino (*Mignani*)

VAN PRAAG, H.: See Praag, H. C. Van

VIERA, BRANDO J.: *CA* Chôre (f. ca. c. b.) (*E.C.I.C.*)

VILLA-LOBOS, H. (20): Quartet (*Eschig*)

VRIES ROBBÉ, W. DE (20): Quartetto (*Donemus*)

WALENTYNOWICZ, W. (20): Quartet (*Moeck*)

WELLESZ, E.: Op. 73 Suite (o. c. h. b.) (*Sikorski*)

WOLF, E. W.: Quartet (f. o. b. vc. or db.) (*Marbot*)

WOLFF, MOSS. L. H.: *CA* Präludium and Fuge (o. ca. va. vc.) (*Donemus*)

ZAGWIJN, H. (20): *CA* Suite (2 o. ca. heck.) (*Donemus*)

ZLATIC, S. (20): *CA* Balun Istarskinarodni Ples (o. ca. alt. sax. b.) (*M. Naklada*)

IV (6) QUARTETS WITH KEYBOARD INSTRUMENT

BENTZON, N. V. (20): Op. 94 *O* Triple Concerto (o. c. b. p.) (*Hansen*)

COUPERIN, F. (17/18): 1 Ère Concert (o. c. b. ce.) (*Delrieu*)

DRESSEL, E.: *O* Concerto (o. c. b. p.) (*Ries & Erler*)

DUNHILL, T. (20): Two Short Pieces (f. or o., v. va. p.) (*Augener*)

FASCH, J. F. (18): Sonata in B flat (f. o. v. bc.) (*Bärenreiter*); Quartet in C (o. 2 v. bc.) (*Sikorski*)

GRUNENWALD, J. J.: Fantaisie Arabesque (o. c. b. p.) (*Salabert*)

HEINICHEN, J. D. (18): Concerto in G (o. 2 v. ce.) (*Vieweg*)

JANITSCH, J. (18): Op. 8 Chamber Sonata 'Echo' (f. o. va. p.) (*Breit-kopf*) See also in Section iv. 4 page 107

KROMMER (KRAMÁŘ), F. (18/19) :Concertante (f. o. v. p.) (*Hofmeister*)

MARTINŮ, B. (20): Quartet (o. v. vc. p.) (*Eschig*)

MILHAUD, D.: Sonata (f. o. c. p.) (*Andraud*)

NAUDOT, J. J. (18): Concerto in G (o. 2 v. bc.) (*Bärenreiter*)

RIETI, V. (20): Sonata (f. o. b. p.) (*Universal*)

ROLAND-MANUEL (20): Suite Dans le Gout Espagnole (o. b. tp. p.) (*Durand*)

SAINT SAËNS, C. (19/20): Op. 79 Caprice sur des Airs Danois et Russes (f. o. c. p.) (*Durand*)

SCARLATTI, A. (17/18): Sonata (3 f. or 3 o. bc.) (*Moeck*)

SCHMITT, F. (19/20): Op. 97 A Tour d'Anches (o. c. b. p.) (*Durand*)

SOURILAS, T.: Suite (o. h. vc. p. or hp.) (*Lemoine*)

SPILER, M.: *CA* Samotni Trenutak (f. ca. c. p.) (*M. Naklada*); Sjetni Trenutak (f. o. bass c. p.) (*M. Naklada*)

STARER, R. (20): 'Cantamus' (o. b. v. p.) (*Israeli*)

STÖLZEL, G. H. (18): Sonata in F minor (o. h. or c., v. p.) (*Breitkopf* or *Nagel*)

TELEMANN, G. P. (18): Quartet in D (o. v. va. bc.) (*Sikorski*); Quartet in G (f. o. v. bc) (*Sikorski* or *Peters*); Quartet in F (f. o. v. p.) (*Schott*); Concerto in A minor (f. o. v. bc.) (*Sikorski*); Quartet in G minor (f. o. vg. or va., bc.) (*Sikorski*)

TOWNSEND (20): Var. on a Theme of Mihaud (f. o. vc. or b. p.) (*Peters*)

ZLATÍC, S. (20): *CA* Balun (o. ca. alt. sax. b.) (*M. Naklada*)

IV   (7) QUINTETS FOR WIND
(flute, oboe, clarinet, horn, bassoon)

ABSIL, J. (20): Op. 16 Quintet and Op. 37 Suite Pastorale (*Cebedem*)

AGAY, D. (20): Five Leichte Tanze (*Universal*)

ALJABJEW, A. A. (20): Quintet (*Russian S.P.H.*)

ANDRIESSEN, H. (20): Quintet (*Donemus*)

ARNELL, R. (20): Cassation (*Peters*)

ARNOLD, M. (20): 3 Shanties (*Paterson*)

ARRIEU (20): Quintet (*Noël*)

ASCHEN BRENNER, J. (20): Quintet (*Modern*)

BACEWICZ, G. (20): Quintet (*Moeck*)

BADINGS, H. (20): Wind Quintet 1 (*Donemus*); Wind Quintet 2 (*Donemus*)

BAEYENS, A. L. (20): Quintet (*Cebedem*)

BALAY (20): Petite Suite Miniature dans le style du 18 ème Siècle (*Leduc*)

BAKALEÌNIKOV, V.: Introduction and Scherzo (*Belwin*)

BARBER, S. (20): Op. 31 Summer Music (*Schirmer*)

BARROWS, J. R.: March (*Schirmer*)

BARTHE (19): Passacaille (*Leduc*)

BARTOS, F. (20): Suite: Le Bourgeois Gentilhomme (*Artia*)

BAUR, J. (20): Quintetto Sereno (*Breitkopf*)

BEEKHUIS, H. (20): Quintet (*Donemus*); Elegie and Humoreske (*Donemus*)

BENNETT, D. (20): Rhapsodette (*Fischer*)

BENTZON, J. (20): Racconto 5 (*Skandinavisk*)

BEREZOWSKY: Op. 11 Suite 1 (*Boosey* (*U.S.A.*)); Op. 22 Suite 2 (*Mills*)

BITSCH, M. (20): Sonatine (*Leduc*)

BLUMER, T. (20): Op. 52 Quintet for Wind (*Zimmermann*); Tanzsuite (*Simrock*); Schweizer Quintet (*Zimmermann*)

BOEDIJN, G. (20): Kwintet Concertante (*Donemus*)

BONSEL, A. (20): Quintet 1 (*Donemus*)

BORCH: Quintet 2 (*De Wolfe*); Sunrise on the Mountains (*Mills*)

BOŘKOVEC, P. (20): Quintet (*Artia*)

BOROWSKI, F.: Madrigal to the Moon (*Boosey*)

BORRIS, S. (20): Op. 25/2 Wind Quintet (*Sirius*)

BOSMANS, A. (20): Diabelliana Suite (*Elkan*)

BOURGIGNON, F. DE: Op. 71 2 Pieces (*Cebedem*)

BOZZA, E. (20): Op. 42 Var. Sur un Thème Libre (*Leduc*); Op. 48 Scherzo (*Leduc*)

BRENTA, G. (20): Soldat Fanfaron (*Cebedem*)

BRICCIALO: Op. 124 Quintet (*Schott*)

BROD, H.: Op. 2/1 Wind Quintet in B flat (*McGinnis*)

BRUGK, H. M.: Op. 22 Serenade (*Sikorski*)

BRUNS, V.: Op. 16 Quintet (*Hofmeister*)

BURIAN, E. F. (20): Quintet (*Artia*)

CAILLET, L.: Concertino for Wind Quintet (*Elkan-Vogel*)

CARTER, E.: Quintet (*A.M.P.*)

CASTÉRÈDE (20): Quintette (*Leduc*)

CAZDEN, N.: 3 Constructions (*Kalmus*)

CHAGRIN, F. (20): Divertimento (*Augener*)

CHAILLEY (20): Barcarolle (*Leduc*)

CHAYNES (20): Serenade (*Leduc*)

CHEMIN-PETIT, H. (20): Quintet (*Lienau*)

CHEVREUILLE, R.: Op. 21 Divertimento (*Cebedem*); Op. 65 Serenade (*Cebedem*)

COHEN, S. B. (20): Suite for Wind Quintet (*Fischer*)

CLAPP, P. G.: Prelude and Finale (*Boosey*)

COLAÇO, O. S. (20): Suite (*Donemus*)

COLOMER (20): Bourrée (*Leduc*)

COOKE, A. (20): Quintet (*Mills*)

COWELL (20): Suite (*Mercury*)

DAHLHOFF, W. (20): The Leuthen Choral (*Schmidt*)

DAMASE, J. M. (20): 17 Variations (*Leduc*)

DANZI, F. (18/19): Op. 56/1 Quintet in B flat (*Leukhart*); Op. 56/2 Quintet in G minor (*Leukhart*); Op. 67/1 Quintet in E minor (*Kneusslin*); Op. 67/2 Quintet in E minor (*Kneusslin*); Op. 86/1 Quintet in A (*Kneusslin*)

DAVID, G. (20): Fúvósötös Quintet (*Kultura*)

DAVID, GYULA (20): Serenade (*Mills*)

DAVID, J. N.: Divertimento Nach Alten Volksliedern (*Breitkopf*)

DEMUTH, N. (20): Pastorale and Scherzo (*Hinrichsen*)

DESSERRÉ, G. T.: Suite (*Marbot*)

DÉSORMIÈRE, R. (20): *CA* 6 Danceries du 16 ème Siècle (*Leduc*)

DOMANSKY, A.: Quintet (*Schmidt*)

DESPORTES, Y.: Prel., Var. and Finale on a Gregorian Chant (*Andraud*)

DOMENICO, O. DI: Quintetto (*Leduc*)

DOUGLAS, R. (20): 6 Dance Caricatures (*Hinrichsen*)

DUBOIS, C.: Première Suite (*Mercury*); Deuxième Suite (*Leduc*)

DUBOIS, P. M. (20): Fantasie (*Leduc*)

ECKARTZ, H.: Quintet (*Iris*)

EDER, H. (20): Op. 25 Wind Quintet (*Doblinger*)

EGGE, K. (20): Wind Quintet (*Lyche*)

EMBORG, G.: Op. 74 Quintet (*Dania*)

ERDLEN, H. (20) Kleine Variationen Über ein Frühlingsleid (*Zimmermann*)

ESSEX, K. (20): Quintet (*Hinrichsen*)

ETLER, A.: Quintet 2 (*A.M.P.*)

FARKAS, F.: Serenade (*Kultura*); Seventeenth century Hungarian Dances (*Kultura*)

FERNANDEZ, O. L.: Suite (*A.M.P.*)

FERNSTRÖM, J.: Op. 59 Quintet (*F.S.T.*)

FINE, I. G.: Partita (*Boosey*)

FINKE, F. (20): Quintet (*Breitkopf*)

FOERSTER, J. B. (19/20): Op. 95 Quintet (*Artia*)

FRAGALE, F.: Quintet (*A.M.P.*)

FRANÇAIX, J. (20): Op. 5 Quintet (*Eschig*)

FREYER, J.: Op. 40 Divertimento für 5 Bläser (*Breitkopf*)

FRICKER, P. R. (20): Op. 5 Quintet (*Schott*)

FÜRST, P. W.: Konzertante Musik (*Doblinger*)

FUSSAN, W.: Op. 14 Quintet (*Kasparek*)

FUSSL: Kleine Kammermusik (*Bärenreiter*)

GADE, N. W.: Merry Go Round (*Elkan*)

GAYFER, J. M.: Suite (*Boosey*)

GEISSLER, F. (20): Heitere Suite (*Breitkopf*)

GENZMER (20): Quintet (*Peters*)

GERAEDTS (20): Kleine Watermusiek (*Donemus*)

GERHARD, R. (20): Wind Quintet (*Mills*)

GERSTER, O.: Heitere Musik (*Schott*)

GHEDINI, F.: Concerto for Five (*Ricordi*)

GILLIS, DON (20): Suite 1 The Fable of the Tortoise and the Hare (*Mills*); Suite 2 Three Sketches (*Mills*); Suite 3 Gone with the Woodwinds (*Mills*)

GOEB, R.: Prairie Songs Quintet (*Southern*)

GOUVY, L. T.: Serenade (*Sikorski*)

GRAINGER, P.: Walking Tune (*Schott*)

GRIMM, C. H.: Op. 36 A Little Serenade (*Southern*)

GROOT, H. DE: Variations (*Broekman*)

HAAS: Op. 10 Suite (*Sadlo*)

HALL, P. (20): Suite (*Lyche*)

HANBIEL, C.: 5 Pieces (*Composers' Press*)

HARTLEY, G. (20): Quintet (*A.M.P.*)

HEIDEN, B.: Sinfonia (*A.M.P.*)

HEIM, M.: Quintet (*Schmidt*)

HEMERIK, E.: Quintet (*Larsen*)

HENKEMANS, H. (20): Kwintet (*Donemus*)

HENZE, H. W. (20): Quintet (*Schott*)

HERMANN, F.: Zur Ubung im Zu (*Breitkopf*)

HESS, W. (20): Op. 51 Divertimento in B flat (*Hinrichsen*)

HILLMAN, K.: Op. 57 Capriccio (*Belwin*)

HINDEMITH, P. (20): Op. 24/2 Kleine Kammermusik (*Schott*)

HIPMAN, S. (20): Op. 11 Čáslaver Suite (*Artia*)

HOFFDING (20): Op. 35 Quintet (*Skandinavisk*)

HÖFFER, P. (20): Variations on a Theme of Beethoven (*Peters*)

HOLBROOKE, J. (19/20): Miniature Characterische Suite (*De Wolfe*)

HOLMBOE, V. (20): Quintet (*Viking*)

HOYER: Op. 29 Serenade in F (*A.M.P.*)

HUNTER: Danse Humoresque (*Fischer*)

HUYBRECHTS, A.: Quintet (*Cebedem*)

IBERT, J. (20): Trois Pieces Brèves (*Leduc*)

INGENHOVEN, J.: Quintet (*Wunderhorn*)

JACOBI, F. (20): Scherzo (*Fischer*)

JACOBY, H. (20): Quintet (*Israeli*)

JAMES, P. (20): Suite (*Fischer*)

I

JÁRDÁNYI, P.: Quintet (*Kultura*)
JERSILD, J.: Serenade (*Hansen*)
JOHNSON, H. (20): Quintet in C (*Fischer*)
JOLIVET (20): Serenade (*Costallat*)
JONGEN: Op. 124 Concerto for Wind Quintet (*Southern*); Op. 98 Preambule and Dances (*Southern*)
JUNGK, K. Chaconne (*Sikorski*)
JUON, P.: Op. 84 Quintet (*Lienau*)
KADOSA, P. (20): 2 Quintets (*Kultura*)
KALLSTENIUS, E.: Divertimento (*F.S.T.*)
KAPP, V.: Suite (*Russian S.P.H.*)
KARKOFF, M.: Op. 25 Quintet (*F.S.T.*)
KAUFFMANN, F.: Op. 40 Quintet (*Heinrichsofen*)
KAUFFMANN, L. J.: Quintet (*Universal*)
KEITH, G. D. (20): Quintet (*Boosey*)
KELTERHORN, R. (20): 7 Bagatellen (*Modern*)
KERN, F.: Quintet (*Grosch*)
KING, H. C. (20): Kwintet (*Donemus*)
KIRBY, S. T. (20): Elfin Dance (*A.M.P.*)
KLUGHARDT, A. (19): Op. 79 Quintet (*Zimmermann*)
KOETSIER, J. (20): Op. 16/1 and Op. 35/1 Divertimenti 1 and 2 (*Donemus*)
KÖHNEL: Quintet (*Grosch*)
KOMMA, K. M. (20): Divertimento (*Ichthys*)
KÖTSCHAU, J.: Op. 14 Quintet (*Zimmermann*)
KRENEK, E. (20): Pentagramm (*Bärenreiter*)
KUBIZEK, A. (20): Kammerquintett (*Breitkopf* or *Doblinger*)
KUNERT, K.: Op. 14 Wind Quintet (*Grosch*); Op. 17 Wind Quintet (*Hofmeister*); Op. 18 Divertimento 2 (*Hofmeister*)
LABATE, B. (20): Intermezzo 2 (*Mills*)
LABEY, M.: Quintet (*Eschig*)
LANDRÉ, G. (20): Quintet (*Donemus*)
LAURISCHKUS, M.: Op. 23 Suite (*Simrock*)
LEFEBVRE, H. (19/20): Suite (*Hamelle*); Suite 2 (*Evette*)
LENDVAL, E.: Op. 23 Quintet (*Simrock*)
LILIEN, I. (20): Quintetto 2 (*Donemus*); Voyage au Printemps (*Donemus*)
LILGE: Op. 67 Variations and Fugue (*Kistner*)
LINDNER: Quintet in B flat (*Hofmeister*)
LORENZO, F.: Op. 37 Quintet (*A.M.P.*)
LOUEL, J. (20): Quintet (*Cebedem*)
LUCKY, S. (20): Wind Quintet (*Artia*)
LUENING, O. (20): Fuguing Tune (*A.M.P.*)
LUTYENS, E. (20): Wind Quintet (*Mills*)

MALIPIERO, G. F. (20): Dialogho 4 (*Ricordi*); Musica da Camera (*Suvini*)
MANDIC: Quintet (*Universal*)
MARECHAL, H.: Air de Guet, Theme Provençal (*Heugel*)
MAROS, R.: Musica Leggiera (*Kultura*)
MARTIN, F.: Prestissimo (*Boosey* (*U.S.A.*))
MASON, D.: Op. 26b Divertimento (*Witmark*)
MEDERACKE, K.: Op. 34 Bohemian Suite (*Hofmeister*)
MEESTER, L. DE (20): Divertimento (*Cebedem*)
MENDELSSOHN, J. ARKO (20): Figurate Hymn (*Fischer*)
MEULEMANS, A.: 2 Quintets (*Cebedem*)
MIGOT, G. (20): Quintette (*Leduc*)
MILHAUD, D. (20): Divertissement (*Heugel*); La Cheminée du Roi René (*Southern*); 2 Sketches (*Mercury*)
MOORE, D. (20): Quintet (*Fischer*)
MORITZ, E. (20): Op. 41 Quintet (*Zimmermann*)
MORTENSEN, FINN (20): Op. 4 Quintet (*Hansen*)
MORTENSEN, OTTO (20): *CA* Quintet (*Hansen*)
MOYZES, A.: Quintet (*Simrock*)
MÜLLER, P. (20): Wind Quintet in E flat (*Mus. Rara*)
NELHYBEL, V.: Quintet (*Eulenberg*)
NEVIN: Gondolieri (*Presser*)
NIELSEN, C. (19/20): Quintet for Wind (*Hansen*)
OLSEN, S. (20): Op. 35 Quintet (*Lyche*)
ONSLOW, G. (19): Op. 81/3 Quintet in F (*Leuckart*)
OTTEN, L. (20): Blaasquintet 2 (*Donemus*)
OUBRADOUS, F. (20): Fantaisie Dialogues (*Oiseau-Lyre*)
PANUFNIK, A.: Quintet (*Polish S.P.H.*)
PARRIS, H. M. (20): Miniatures (*Elkan*)
PESSARD: Op. 6 Aubade (*Leduc*); Prélude et Menuet du Capitaine Fracasse (*Leduc*)
PERSICHETTI, V.: Op. 21 Pastoral (*Schirmer*)
PIERCE: Allegro Piacevole and Scherzo (*Remick*)
PIERNÉ, P. (20): Op. 14 Suite Pittoresque (*Leduc*)
PIJPER, W. (20): Quintet (*Donemus*)
PISTON, W. (20): Quintet (*A.M.P.*)
PONSE, L. (20): Deux Pièces (*Donemus*)
PORSCH: Suite Modique (*Remick*)
PRAAG, H. C. VAN (20): Kwintet (1938) (*Donemus*); Quintet (1948) (*Donemus*)
QUINET, M.: Quintet (*Cebedem*); 8 Petites Pièces (*Cebedem*)
RANDERSON: Quintet (*Durand*)
RANKI, G.: Pentaerophonia, 3 Pieces (*Kultura*)
RAPOPORT, E.: Indian Legend (*A.M.P.*)

RATHAUS, K.: Galante Serenade (*Boosey*)

READ, G. (20): Scherzino (*Southern*)

REICHA, A. (18/19): Op. 88/2 Quintet in E flat (*Leukhart*); Op. 88/3 Quintet in G (*Artia*); Op. 88/5 Quintet in B flat (*Leukhart*); Op. 91/1 Quintet in C (*Kneusslin*); Op. 91/3 Quintet in D (*Kneusslin*); Op. 91/9 Quintet in D (*Artia*); Op. 91/11 Quintet in A (*Artia*); Op. 100/4 Quintet in E minor (*Kneusslin*)

REIZENSTEIN, F. (20): Quintet (*Boosey*)

RENZI, A. (20): 5 Bagatelles (*Di Santis*)

REVUELTAS, S. (20): Suite (*Southern*)

RIEGGER, W. (20): Op. 51 Wind Quintet (*Schott*)

ROIKJER, K. Quintet (*Skandinavisk*)

ROPARTZ, G. (19/20): Deux Pièces (*Durand*)

RORICH, K. (19/20): Op. 58 Quintet (*Zimmermann*)

ROSETTI, A. (18): CA Quintet (*Kneusslin*)

ROSSEAU, N. (20): Op. 54 Quintet (*Cebedem*)

ROTA, N. (20): Petite Offrande Musicale (*Leduc*)

RUYNEMAN, D. (20): Nightingale Quintet (*Donemus*)

SACHSSE: Op. 32 Suite in C (*Boehm*)

SCHAT, P. (20): Improvisations and Symphonies (*Donemus*)

SCHIERBECK, P.: Op. 53 Capriccio (*Hansen*)

SCHINDLER, G.: Divertimento Notturno (*Modern*)

SCHISKE, K. (20): Op. 24 Wind Quintet (*Doblinger*)

SCHMID, H. K. (19/20): Op. 28 Quintet (*Schott*)

SCHMITT, F. (19/20): Op. 125 Chants Alizés (*Durand*)

SCHÖNBERG, A. (19/20): Op. 26 Quintet (*Universal*)

SCHOUWMAN, H. (20): Op. 40b Nederlandse Suite (*Donemus*)

SCHULLER, G. Suite for Wind (*McGinnis*)

SCHULTZ, S.: Petite Serenade (*Skandinavisk*)

SCHWARTZ, L.: Oriental Suite (*Universal*)

SCHWEITZER, A. (19/20): Quintet (*Sikorski*)

SEHLBACH, E. (20): Op. 30 Kortum Serenade (*Möseler*)

SEIBER, M. (20): Permutazioni a Cinque (*Schott*)

SEREBRIER, J.: Little Suite (*Southern*)

SZERVÁNSKY, E.: 2 Wind Quintets (*Kultura*)

SMETACEK, V.: Suite (*Continental*)

SOBECK, J.: Op. 11 and 14 2 Quintets (*Bosworth*)

SODERO, C.: Morning Prayer (*A.M.P.*)

SOURIS, A. (20): Rengaines (*Leduc*)

SOWERBY, L. (20): Quintet (*Fischer*)

STAINER, C. (20): Scherzo (*Boosey*)

STONE, D.: Prelude and Scherzetto (*Novello*)

STRONG, G. T.: 5 Acquarelles (*Siècle Musicale*)

SUSATO/BONSEL (16/20): Old Dutch Dances (*De Wolfe*)

SZALOWSKI, A. (20): Wind Quintet (*Ars Polona (Omega)*)

SZEKELY, E. (20): Wind Quintet (*Mills*)

SZELIGOWSKY, T. (20): Quintet (*Moeck*)

TAFFANEL, P. (19/20): Quintette (*Leduc*)

TAYLOR, L.: Little Suite (from eighteenth-century composers) (*Mills*)

TELEMANN, G. P. (18): Ouverturen Suite (also for 2 o. 2 h. b.) (*Leukhart*)

THILMAN, J. P. (20): Op. 44 Wind Quintet (*Peters*)

TIESSEN, H.: Op. 51 Divertissement (*Kistner*)

TOEBOSCH, L. (20): Sarabande and Allegro (*Donemus*)

TOMASI, H. (20): Var. sur un Thème Corse and Quintet (*Leduc*)

TREXLER, G.: Spitzweg Suite (*Breitkopf*)

TROJAN (20): Op. 8 Wind Quintet (*Artia*)

TURECHEM: Introduction and Scherzo (*Witmark*)

TUTHILL, B. (20): Op. 11/1 Sailor's Hornpipe (*Fischer*)

VALEN, F. (20): Op. 42 Serenade (*Lyche*)

VELDEN, R. VAN DER (20): 2nd Concerto for Wind Quintet (*Metropolis*)

VERRALL, J.: Serenade (*Mercury*)

VINTER, G. (20): Two Miniatures (*Boosey*)

VREDENBURG, M. (20): Suite Brève (Au Pays des Vendanges) (*Donemus*)

VLIJMEN, J. VAN (20): Quintet (*Donemus*)

WARD: Little Dance Suite (*Mills*)

WEBER, A.: Quintette (*Leduc*)

WEIS, F. (20): Serenade Without Serious Intentions (*Hansen*)

WELLESZ, E. (20): Op. 73 Suite (*Sikorski*)

WHETTAM, G. (20): Op. 19 Wind Quintet (*De Wolfe*)

WIJDEVELD, W. (20): Quintet (*Donemus*)

WILDER, A. (20): Wind Quintet 3 (*Schirmer*)

WILDSCHUT, C.: Kleine Serenade (*Donemus*)

WIRTH, H.: Kleine Clementiade (Scherzo) (*Sikorski*)

WOESTYNE, D. VAN DE (20): Musique pour cinq instr. (*Cebedem*)

WOOD, C. (19/20): Quintet in F for Wind (*Boosey*)

ZAGWIJN, H. (19/20): Quintet (*Donemus*)

ZENDER, H. (20): Op. 3 Quintet (*Böte & Bock*)

ZILCHER, H. (20): Op. 91 Quintet (*Müller*)

IV (8) SEXTETS FOR WIND QUINTET AND KEYBOARD INSTRUMENT

ANDRIESSEN, J. (20): L'incontro di Cesare e Cleopatra (*Donemus*)

BADINGS, H. (20): Sextet (*Donemus*)

BLUMER, T. (20): Sextet: Kammersinfonie (*Ries & Erler*)

BOISDEFFRE, C. (19): Sextet (*Hamelle*)

BRAUER: Sextet in C (*A.M.P.*)

BURLINGHAME HILL, E. (20): Sextet (*S.P.A.M.*)

DAVID, J. N.: Op. 24 Divertimento (*Breitkopf*)

D'INDY, V. (19/20): Op. 24 bis. Sarabande et Menuet (*Hamelle*)

DRESDEN, S. (20): works include Suite after Rameau (*De Wolfe*)

DUKELSKY (20): Nocturne (*Fischer*)

FRENSEL WEGENER, E. (20): Sextet (*Donemus*)

FÜHRMEISTER, F. (19/20): Gavotte and Tarantella (*Zimmermann*)

GENIN, T.: Sextet (*Eschig*)

GODRON, H. (20): Serenade (*Donemus*)

GÖRNER (20): Op. 29 Kammerkouzest Sextet (*Peters*)

HILL, E. B.: Op. 39 Sextet (*Schirmer*)

HOLBROOKE, J. (19/20): Sextet (*Modern Music Lib.*)

JACOB, G. (20): Sextet (*Musica Rara*)

JENTSCH, W.: Op. 5 Kleine Kammermusik (*Ries & Erler*)

JONGEN, J. (19/20): Op. 70 Rhapsody (*Cebedem*)

JUON, P. (19/20): Op. 51 Divertimento (*Lienau*)

KOPPEL, H. (20): Sextet (*Skandinavisk*)

LADMIRAULT, P.: Choral et Variations (*Lemoine*)

LEGLEY, V.: Op. 19 Sextet (*Cebedem*)

MEULEMANS, A.: Aubade (*Cebedem*)

MILLER, R. D.: 3 American Dances (*Fischer*)

MOULAERT, R.: Sextet (*Cebedem*)

MULDER, E. W.: Sextet (*Donemus*)

OSIECK, H. (20): Divertimento (*Donemus*)

PIJPER, W. (20): Sextet (*Donemus*); Phantasie (W. A. Mozart) (*Donemus*)

POULENC, F. (20): Sextet (*Hansen*)

QUEF: Op. 4 Sextet (*Noël*)

REUCHSEL, A. (20): Sextet (*Lemoine*)

RHEINBERGER: Op. 191B Sextet (*Leuchart*)

RICCI SIGNORINI, A.: Fantasia Burlesca (*Carisch*)

RIEGGER, W. (20): Op. 53 Concerto: Piano and Wind Quintet (*A.M.P.*)

RIJSAGER, K.: Op. 28a Concerto for Wind Quintet and Piano (*Nordiska*)

ROOS, R. DE (20): Sextuor (*Donemus*)

ROUSSEL, A. (19/20): Op. 6 Divertissement (*Rouart*)

SCHROEDER, H.: Op. 36 Sextet (*Schott*)

SEIDEL, L. (20): Sextet (ce. or p.) (*De Wolfe*)

SHANKS, E.: Night Music for Sextet (*Gamble*)

SMIT, L. (20): Sextuor (*Donemus*)

STRATEGIER, H. (20): Sextet (*Donemus*)

TANSMAN, A. (20): Witches' Dance (*Eschig*)

THUILLE, L. (19): Op. 6 Sextet (*Breitkopf*)
TUTHILL, B. (20) Op. 9 Variations (*Galaxy*)
WHETTAM, G. (20) Op. 19 Fantasy Sextet (*De Wolfe*)
WINNUBST, J. (19/20): Kleine Serenade (*Donemus*)
ZAGWIJN, H. (20): Scherzo and Suite (*Donemus*)

IV   (9)   OBOE AND STRINGS
(Unless otherwise stated, Quartet = Oboe, Violin, Viola, Cello;
         Quintet = Oboe, 2 Violins, Viola, Cello)

ABEL, C. F. (18): Op. 12/2 Quartet in A (*Musica Rara*)
BACH, J. C. (18): Op. 8/1 Quartet in C (*Dunnebeil*); Op. 8/2 Quartet
     (*Musica Rara*); Quartets 1, 3, 5 (*Bärenreiter*)
BALORRE (20): Trio (o. va. vc.) (*Hamelle*)
BAX, A. (20): Quintet (*Chappell*)
BLISS, A. (20): Quintet (*O.U.P.*)
BOCCHERINI, L. (18): Op. 21/1, 2, 3, 4, 5, 6 Quintets in D, C, D, B♭,
     G, E♭ (*Mus. Rara*); Op. 45/4, 5, 6 Quintets in A, E♭, D minor
     (*Sikorski*)
BORRIS, S. (20): Op. 17/1 Quartet (*Sirius*); Op. 45/1 Sonatina per tre
     (o. v. va.) (*Sirius*)
BRITTEN, B. (20): Op. 2 Phantasy Quartet (*Boosey*)
BOURGIGNON, F. DE: Op. 100 Quintet (*Cebedem*)
CADOW: Var. on a Swedish Folk-Song (Quintet) (*Grosch*)
CHERUBINI, L. (18/19): *CA* Two Sonatas (ca. and str. quartet)
     (*Sikorski*)
COLE, H. (20): Quartet (*Novello*)
COOKE, A. (20): Quartet (*Novello*)
CRUFT, A. (20): Fantasy Quartet (*Williams*)
CRUSELL: Op. 9 Divertimentio (quintet) (*Peters*)
EMBORG, J. L.: Op. 55b 3 Short Pieces (o. va. vc.) (*Larsen*)
FASCH, J. F. Quartet in C (*Sikorski*)
FECKÉR, A.: Liedvariationen (o. 2 v.) (*Möseler*)
FINZI, G. (20): Interlude (quintet) (*Boosey*)
HAYDN, J. (18): Divertissement (quartet, opt. ce.) (*O.U.P.*)
HAYDN, M. (18): *CA* Quartet in C (ca. v. va. vc.) (*Sikorski*)
HENNESSY, W. S. (19/20): *CA* 4 Celtic Pieces (ca. v. va. vc.) (*Eschig*)
HERMANS, N. (20): Op. 3 Serenade (quartet) (*Donemus*)
HÖFFER, P. (20): Serenade (quartet) (*Peters*)
HONEGGER, A. (20): *CA* Choral (Contrepoint 2) (ca. va. vc.) (*Hansen*)
HOROVITZ, J. (20): Op. 18 Quartet (*Mills*)
JACOB, A. (20): Quartet (*Novello*)
KAUN, B. (20): Quintet (*Jupiter*)
KENNAWAY, L.: *P* Interrupted Serenade (quintet, opt. p.) (*Hin-
     richsen*)

KOETSEIR, J. (20): *CA* Quintet (ca and str. quartet) (*Donemus*)

KOTSCHAU, J. (20): Divertimento 2 (o. va. vc.) (*Zimmermann*)

KOPPEL, H. (20): Op. 61 Divertimento (o. va. vc.) (*Dania*)

KROMMER (KRAMÁŘ), F. (18/19): Two Quartets (*Artia*)

KROL, B. (20): Op. 9 Quartet (*Marbot*)

MAASZ, G. (20): Divertimento (quintet) (*Sikorski*)

MCBRIDE, R. (20): Op. 40 Quintet (*Schirmer*)

MILHAUD, D. (20): Les Rêves de Jacob (o. v. va. vc. db.) (*Heugel*)

MILNER, A.: Quartet (*Novello*)

MORTARI, V. (20): 3 Old Dances (quartet) (*Carisch*)

MOZART, W. A. (18): K. 370 *P* Quartet in F (*Breitkopf* or *Boosey* or *Chester*); *CA* K. ahn. 2. 94 Adagio (ca. and str. quartet) (*Kasparek*)

RACEK, F.: Eine Kleine Hausmusik (o. v. va.) (*Doblinger*)

REICHA, A. (18/19): Quintet (*Simrock*)

SCHLEMM, G. A. *P* Pastorale and Scherzo (quintet) (*Zimmermann*)

SHAFFER, S. J.: Quintet (*Fischer*)

SHIELD, W. (18/19): Op. 3/2 Quartet in F (*Schott*)

STAMITZ, K. (18): Op. 4/6 Quartet in A (*Leukhart*); Op. 8/1 Quartet in D (*Bärenreiter*); Op. 8/3 Quartet in E flat (*Mus. Rara* or *Sikorski*); Op. 8/4 Quartet in E flat (*Mus. Rara* or *Peters*); Two Quartets in D and A (*McGinnis*)

STRATEGIER, H. (20): Drie Stukken (quintet) (*Donemus*)

SUCK, CHARLES J. (18): Trio 1 in C major (o. v. vc.) (*Chester*)

VANHALL, J. B. (18/19): Quartet 7 (*Mus. Rara*)

WORDSWORTH, W. (20): Op. 44 Quartet (*Lengnick*)

ZECHLIN, R.: Trio (o. va. vc.) (*Peters*)

IV (10) OBOE AND VOICE, WITH ONE OR TWO OTHER INSTRUMENTS

BACH, J. S. (18): Ausgewählte Arien (*Breitkopf*). Several volumes of solo arias from choral works, with separate parts for voice, obbligato instrument and piano reduction.

BADINGS, H. (20): Drie Geestelijk Liederen (alt. o. org.) (*Donemus*)

BEDFORD, H. (19/20): Night Piece 2. The Shepherd (voice, f. o. p.) (*S. & B*)

BIVANCH, H. (20): Twee Liederen (alt. o. org.) (*Donemus*)

BOWLES, P. F. (20): Anabase (voice, o. p.) (*New Music*)

BURKHART, F. (20): Drei Adventlieder (med. voice, o. g.) (*Doblinger*)

CROFT, W. (18): Cantata: Celladon (sop. o. p.) (*Schott*)

DIJK, J. VAN (20): 6 Liederen (alt. o. org.) (*Donemus*)

FLOTHUIS, M. (20): Op. 49 Negro Lament (alt. o. p.) (*Donemus*)

HANDEL, G. F. (18): She's Gone Guardian Angels (sop. o. p.) (*Broekmans*); Chi T'Intende (sop. o. p.) (*Broekmans*); Liebliche

Walder (from Almira) (voice, o. p.) (*Böte & Bock*); Cara Sposa (from Rinaldo) (voice, o. p.) (*Böte & Bock*)

HINDEMITH, P. (20): Barcarolle (sop. o. vc.) (*Schott*); Nur Mut (sop. o. va.) (*Schott*); Der Abend (sop. o.) (*Schott*); Die Serenaden (sop. o. va. vc.) (*Schott*)

JOLIVET, A. (20): *CA* Suite Liturgique (ten. or sop. o./ca. vc. hp.) (*Durand*)

LEWKOVITCH, B.: Tre Orationes (ten. o. b.) (*Hansen*)

LIER, B. VAN (20): *O d'am* 3 Oud Perzische Kwatrijnen (sop. o. d'am. alt. f. p.) (*Donemus*)

LOHSE, F.: Lyrisches Brevier (med. voice, o. va.) (*Breitkopf*)

LOTHAR, M.: Op. 47 Oboen Lieder (voice, o. p.) (*Ries & Erler*)

NAPIER MILES, P. (19/20): Four Songs (bar. o.) (*O.U.P.*)

OBOUSSIER, R.: 3 Arias (col. sop. o. ce.) (*Bärenreiter*)

POSER, H.: Op. 18/1 Komnt ein Kindlein (sop. f. o. p.) (*Sikorski*)

PURCELL, H. (17): Aria: Bid the Virtues (sop. o. p.) (*Schott*)

SCHMID, R.: 10 Mädchenlieder (sop. o. p.) (*Doblinger*)

SCHOUWMAN, H. (20): Looft God den Heer (high voice, o. p. or org.) (*Donemus*); Oasen Liederencyclus (alt. o. p.) (*Donemus*)

SCOTT, C. (20): Idyllic Fantasy (voice, o. p.) (*Elkin*)

SEHLBACH, E. (20): Eine Kleine Weinachtskantate (sop. f. o. vc.) (*Möseler*)

SIMON, H.: Fünf Plattdeutsche Stucke (mid-voice, o. c. p.) (*Lienau*)

VAUGHAN WILLIAMS, R. (19/20): 10 Blake Songs (ten. o.) (*O.U.P.*)

IV (11) QUINTETS AND LARGER WORKS FOR VARIOUS COMBINATIONS OF INSTRUMENT

In order to save space I have omitted a detailed list for this section, with the few exceptions given below. Players wishing to make their own inquiries may find it helpful to consult the Kammermusic Katalog by Altmann and its continuation (to 1958) compiled by Richter, both published by Hofmeister.

A SHORT LIST OF WELL-KNOWN WORKS

BEETHOVEN, L. VAN (18/19): Op. 16 Quintet in E flat (o. c. h. b. p.) (*Breitkopf* or *Mus. Rara*); Op. 103 Octet (2 o. 2 c. 2 h. 2 b.) (*Sikorski*); Op. 146 Rondino (2 o. 2 c. 2 h. 2 b.) (*Breitkopf*)

DVOŘÁK, A. (19): Serenade (2 o. 2 c. 2 h. 3 h. contra b. vc. db.) (*Mus. Rara*)

HAYDN, J. (18): *O* Symphony Concertante (v. o. vc. b. p.) (*Breitkopf*)

MOZART, W. A. (18): K. 452 Quintet in E flat (o. c. h. b. p.) (*Breitkopf* or *Mus. Rara*); K. anh. 9 *O* Symphony Concertante (o. c. h. b. p.) (*Breitkopf*)

A SHORT LIST OF CLASSICAL COMPOSERS WHOSE WORKS MAY
REPAY EXPLORATION (publishers given in alphabetical order).

BACH, J. C. (18): Quintets and larger works for wind, also for wind
and strings and keyboard instrument (*Bärenreiter, Mus. Rara,
Nagel, Schott*)

BOCCHERINI, L. (18): As above (*Eulenberg, Hofmeister, Mus. Rara,
Novello, Sikorski*)

DITTERSDORF, D. VON (18): Quintets for wind (*Breitkopf, Mus. Rara,
Sikorski*)

HAYDN, J. (18): Several wind sextets, wind octets, and other works
for wind and strings (*Doblinger, Mus. Rara*)

MOZART, W. A. (18): Several serenades and divertimenti for wind
(*Breitkopf, Mus. Rara*); Adagio and rondo (K. 617) for glass
harmonica, f. o. va. vc. (*Breitkopf*)

SPOHR, L. (19): Op. 31 Nonet (v. va. vc. db. f. o. c. h. b.) (*Peters*)

STRAUSS, R. (19/20): Serenade for wind (2 f. 2 o. 2 c. 4 h. 2 b. contra
b.) (*Universal*)

TELEMANN, G. P. (18): Works include wind sextets (*Breitkopf, Leukhart,
Mus. Rara, Sikorski*)

VIVALDI, A. (17/18): Works include many concerti and concerted
works for wind with strings and with cembalo (*Mus. Rara,
Ricordi*)

LIST OF PUBLISHERS REFERRED TO IN APPENDIX III
SHOWING THEIR NATIONALITIES

ALFRED MUSIC CO. U.S.A.

ALSBACH Holland

AMPHION France

AMPHION *now* RICORDI Italy

ANDRAUD *now* SOUTHERN MUSIC
PUBLISHING CO. U.S.A.

ARCADIA U.K.

ARROW U.S.A.

ARS POLONA Poland

ARTIA Czechoslovakia

ASSOCIATED MUSIC PUBLISHERS
U.S.A.

AUGENER U.K.

BAROCK MUS. FULDA U.K.

BÄRENREITER Germany

BELWIN U.S.A.

BESSEL U.K.

BETTONY U.S.A.

BONGIOVANNI Italy

BOOSEY & HAWKES U.K. and
U.S.A.

BÖTE & BOCK Germany

BROEKMANS & VAN POPPEL
Holland

BREITKOPF & HÄRTEL Germany

BROGNEAUX Belgium

BROUDE U.S.A.

BUFFET CRAMPON *now* LEDUC
France

CARISCH Italy

CESKY HUDEBNI (ARTIA) Czechoslovakia

CEBEDEM Belgium

CHANT DU MONDE France

CHESTER U.K.
CHOUDENS France
COMPOSERS' PRESS U.S.A.
CONTINENTALE Czechoslovakia
COSTALLAT France
DANIA Denmark
DE LACOUR *now* LEDUC France
DELRIEU France
DE SANTIS Italy
DE WOLFE U.K.
DÖBLINGER Germany
DONEMUS Holland
DUNNEBEIL Germany
DURDILLY *now* LEDUC France
DURAND France
EASTMAN (FISCHER) U.S.A.
E.C.I.C. Uruguay
ELKAN U.S.A.
ELKAN VOGEL U.S.A.
ENOCH U.K.
ELKIN U.K.
ESCHIG France
EVETTE & SCHAEFFER *now* LEDUC France
EULENBERG Germany
FISCHER U.S.A.
FOETISCH Switzerland
FORBERG Germany
FORLIVESI Italy
FRANCIS, DAY, & HUNTER U.K.
F.S.T. Sweden
GAUDET *now* SALABERT France
GALAXY U.S.A.
GALLET France
GAMBLE U.S.A.
GEHRMANS Sweden
GERVAN Belgium
GOODWIN & TABB U.K.
HAMELLE France
HEINRICHSHOFEN Germany
HANSEN Denmark
HENN Switzerland
HEUWEKEMEYER (DONEMUS) Holland

HINRICHSEN U.K.
HOFMEISTER Germany
HOHNER Germany
ICHTHYS Germany
ISRAELI MUSIC PUBLICATIONS Israel
KAHNT Germany
KALMUS U.K.
KASPAREK Germany
KISTNER & SIEGEL Germany
KNEUSSLIN Switzerland
KOBTRA Czechoslovakia
KUNDELIK Czechoslovakia
KULTURA Hungary
LARSEN Norway
LEDUC France
LEMOINE France
LENGNICK U.K.
LEUKHART Germany
LIENAU E. Germany
LITOLFF *now* PETERS
LYCHE Norway
MCGINNIS & MARX U.S.A.
MARBOT *now* HOFMEISTER Germany
MAURER Belgium
MERCURY U.S.A.
METROPOLIS Belgium
MIGNANI Italy
MILLS MUSIC U.S.A.
MITTELDEUTSCHER E. Germany
MOECK Germany
MODERN Germany
MODERN MUSIC LIBRARY U.K.
MÖSELER Germany
MUSICUS U.S.A.
MÜLLER Germany
MUSICA RARA U.K.
MUS. AKADEMIE LIB. Sweden
MUZIČKA NAKLADA Czechoslovakia
NAGEL Germany
NEW WIND MUSIC CO. U.K.
NOEL-GALLET France

NORDISKA MUSIKFÖRLAGET Sweden

OESTERREICHISCHER BUNDERS-VERLAG Austria

OISEAU-LYRE France

OTTO Czechoslovakia

OXFORD UNIVERSITY PRESS U.K.

PATERSONS PUBLICATIONS U.K.

PEER U.S.A.

PETERS Germany

PHILIPO-GALLET France

POLISH STATE PUBLISHING HOUSE Poland

THEODORE PRESSER U.S.A.

PROCURÉ DU CLERGÉ France

PRO MUSICA E. Germany

KEITH PROWSE U.K.

REMICK U.S.A.

RICHLI Switzerland

RICORDI Italy

RIES & ERLER Germany

ROLLAND now LEDUC France

ROUART now SALABERT France

RUMANIAN STATE PUBLISHING HOUSE Rumania

RUSSIAN STATE PUBLISHING HOUSE U.S.S.R.

SÁDLO Czechoslovakia

SALABERT France

SCHIRMER U.S.A.

SCHMIDT Germany

SCHOTT U.K. and Germany

SCHUBERTH Germany

SELMER U.K. and France

SENART now SALABERT France

SIDEM Switzerland

SIÈCLE MUSICALE Switzerland

SIKORSKI Germany

SIMROCK Germany

SIRIUS Germany

SKANTON E. Germany

SKANDINAVISK MUSIKFORLAG Denmark

SOUTHERN MUSIC CO. U.S.A.

SOUTHERN MUSIC PUBLISHING CO. U.K.

S.P.A.M. (FISCHER) U.S.A.

STAINER & BELL U.K.

STEINGRABER Germany

SUVINI-ZERBONI Italy

UNION MUSICAL ESPAGNOLA (AMP) S. America (U.S.A.)

UNITED MUSIC PUBLISHERS U.K.

UNIVERSAL EDITION U.K. and Austria

URBENEK Czechoslovakia

VALLEY U.S.A.

VIEWEG Germany

VIKING Scandinavia (U.S.A.)

WEINTRAUB U.S.A.

JOSEPH WILLIAMS U.K.

WITMARK U.S.A.

WUNDERHORN now DISCHER-JAGENBERG Germany

ZANIBON Italy

ZIMMERMANN Germany

Date Due